The Formac Pocketguide to

Prince Edward Island
Birds

130 Inland and Shore Birds

Written & illustrated by
Jeffrey C. Domm

Formac Publishing Company Limited
Halifax, Nova Scotia
2002

Dedicated to Jesse and Simeon, for their love of the outdoors.

Formac Publishing Company Limited acknowledges the support of the Cultural Affairs Section, Nova Scotia Department of Tourism and Culture. We acknowledge the financial support of the Government of Canada through the Book Publishing Industry Development Program (BPIDP) for our publishing activities. We acknowledge the support of the Canada Council for the Arts for our publishing program.

National Library of Canada Cataloguing in Publication Data

Domm, Jeff, 1958-
    Formac pocketguide to Prince Edward Island birds

(Formac pocketguide)
ISBN 0-88780-558-2

1. Birds—Prince Edward Island—Identification. 2. Bird watching—Prince Edward Island—Guidebooks. I. Title. II. Series.

QL685.5.P75D65 2002   598'.09717   C2002-901082-9

Cartography by Peggy McCalla

We are grateful to naturalists Dan MacAskill and Ray Cooke for professional advice on the contents of the book in the selection of the hot-spot birding locations.

Formac Publishing Company Limited
5502 Atlantic Street
Halifax, Nova Scotia
Canada B3H 1G4
www.formac.ca

Printed and bound in Canada

Introduction

Affectionately known as the Garden of the Gulf, Prince Edward Island is an ideal landscape for birdwatching. Its softly rolling landscape, magnificent beaches and tidal rivers are easily accessible by the many roads that criss-cross the Island. A short trip will take in many different bird habitats and birders can see a wide variety of species in just a morning. During migration periods, the beaches and tidal flats are especially good for viewing shore and water birds, while spring and autumn bring large numbers of Canada Geese, Black Ducks, gulls, blackbirds, and many other species to farmers' fields. For some suggested birding locations, turn to pages 6-11.

Of the more than 300 species recorded in Prince Edward Island, we have selected 130 familiar and, in a few cases, unusual birds for this book. They are organized in sequence according to the practice of the American Ornithological Union. Each bird is portrayed with an original illustration which is drawn from several sources, including photographs, observations and scientific data. These illustrations emphasize the key features — shape, colour, markings and size — and each one represents a typical specimen. Making an exact match can be tricky: both seasonal changes and varying light conditions affect the appearance of a bird's colouring. For more information on how to identify birds, turn to page 4.

Before setting out on a birdwatching excursion, check tide tables and weather forecasts. Storms can move in quickly bringing strong winds and much cooler temperatures, even in summer. These changes can affect the number of birds you see, not to mention dampen your spirits.

Birds of all sizes play an important role in the balance of nature but they must struggle against unnatural incursions. Preserving habitat diversity is becoming increasingly important as human encroachment extends further into wildlands. Wetlands have declined because of drainage, farming and urbanization. Forests have been harvested and the land used for housing, roads and industrial development. In addition, habitat has been affected by exotic diseases, insects and invasive plants. Many bird species have expanded their ranges due to the loss of habitat, while other species have been reduced in numbers, or lost completely.

The Island Nature Trust and the Natural History Society of Prince Edward Island are two of the Island's public organizations that concern themselves with habitat conservation and education. You can find out more about these and other Island organizations at www.gov.pe.ca, or write to the Island Nature Trust, P.O. Box 265, Charlottetown, P.E.I., C1A 7K4, or to the Natural History Society of Prince Edward Island, P.O. Box 2346, Charlottetown, P.E.I., C1A 8C1.

How to use this guide

Birds don't stay in one place for very long, so it is important to learn a few simple rules to help you identify them quickly. Most often what you see is a bird that is feeding; perhaps it is hopping along the ground or flitting from branch to branch. Maybe it is perched in a tree, preparing to fly away at any second. The visual keys given in this guide focus on the most identifiable features of each bird — colour, outline and size. In addition there are other behavioural traits that help identify birds at a distance. For inland birds nesting location is an important indicator of habitat. For shore and water birds, the way the bird feeds and the style of flying are helpful hints.

When you are looking at a bird first estimate the size, then take note of the shape of the wings, tail, head, beak and feet. Note any particular marks — patches, streaks, stripes and speckles. Watch its movements to see how it flies, hops and feeds.

The index on pages 142-3 is arranged to help you find a bird by size and colour and an index by names follows on page 144.

Legend for visual keys

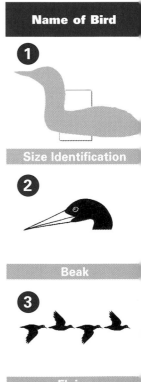

1 **Size identification** — the rectangle represents the page of this book, and the silhouette of the bird represents its size against this page.

2 **Beaks** — the shape of the beak and head can be very helpful in identifying a bird.

3 **Flight characteristics** —

Quick wingbeats

Slow steady wingbeats

Soaring

Wingbeats followed by gliding

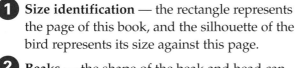

4 **Feeding technique** —

Stabs and prodding motion

Grazing and dabbling

Diving and clutching with feet

Diving head first

Dives from water's surface

Tip up feeding

Skims water surface

Feeding

5 **Backyard Feeder** — there are two types of bird feeder to which small birds might be attracted.

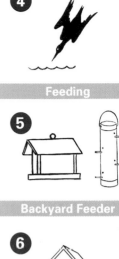

Backyard Feeder

6 **Birdhouse Nester** — some species are happy to make their nest in a manmade house which you might hang in your garden.

Birdhouse Nester

7 **Nesting location** (for inland birds only) —

▼ Hollow in ground

▼ Waterside plants

▽ Bushes and thickets

▼ Cavities of trees

▼ Deciduous trees

▽ Conifers and tall trees

▼ Tall, dead, decaying trees

▽ Banks along rivers and ponds

▽ Cliffs and/or rocky ledges

Nesting Location

8 **Egg** — actual size and shape unless otherwise indicated.

9 **Observation Calendar** — the bar gives the initial for each of the twelve months of the year. The deeper colour indicates the best months for seeing the species, according to known migration patterns.

Observation Calendar
J F M A M J J A S O N D

Egg: 75%

5

Prince Edward Island Birding HOT SPOTS

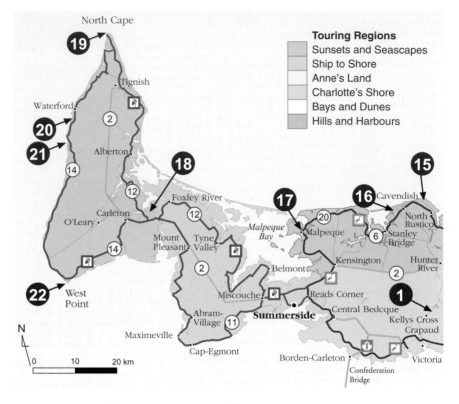

Touring Regions
Sunsets and Seascapes
Ship to Shore
Anne's Land
Charlotte's Shore
Bays and Dunes
Hills and Harbours

Charlotte's Shore

❶ Brookvale Nordic Ski Park

Blue Heron Scenic Drive. Part of the Provincial Forest, it is a great site for woodland birds including warblers, thrushes, woodpeckers, finches, flycatchers, and sparrows as well as hawks and owls. Utilize the park's excellent 15-km nordic ski trail network. On Route 13 northeast of Crapaud.

❷ Ellen's Creek

Blue Heron Scenic Drive. Good waterfowl viewing on a salt marsh on the outskirts of Charlottetown; best in autumn, winter and spring. Gulls, waterfowl, and shorebirds. On the outskirts of Charlottetown near the TransCanada Highway lying adjacent to North River and Beach Grove Roads. Part of Charlottetown's Routes for Nature and Health trail system, which will take you to nearby groves of trees.

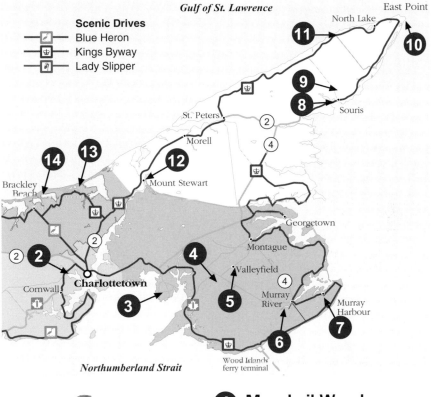

Scenic Drives

——⟋—— Blue Heron
——⚓—— Kings Byway
——⚐—— Lady Slipper

Gulf of St. Lawrence

East Point

North Lake

11
10
9
8

St. Peters
Souris

Morell
2
4

14 **13** **12**

Mount Stewart

Brackley
Beach

Georgetown

2 **2**

Montague

Cornwall
Charlottetown
3
4
Valleyfield
4
5
Murray
River
Murray
Harbour
7
6

Northumberland Strait
Wood Islands
ferry terminal

Hills & Harbours

③ Earnscliffe Peninsula

Kings Byway Scenic Drive. The peninsula features sightings of a variety of woodland and coastal birds including Snow Buntings, Horned Lark and raptors in winter and Whimbrel in late summer. Route 270 off the TransCanada Highway (Route 1). Roadside parking.

④ Macphail Woods Ecological Forestry Project

Kings Byway Scenic Drive. Sightings of woodland birds including thrushes and Barred Owl are possible along the excellent trail system at Macphail Homestead. A pleasant lunch can be had at the homestead or you can visit the Macphail Woods Nature Centre. This site is located near Orwell Historic Village. Turn northeast off Route 1 at Orwell and follow the signs past the historic village. Park at Macphail Homestead.

5 Valleyfield Demonstration Woodlot

Kings Byway Scenic Drive. Woodland birds including warblers, thrushes, vireos, grosbeaks, flycatchers, and chickadees can be sighted along the self-guided wooded interpretive trails of this popular birding site. From Montague take Route 326 southwest to the junction with Route 354 at Valleyfield. Turn right and proceed to the small parking area in the woodlot on the west side of Route 354.

6 MacLure's Pond and Trail, Murray River

Kings Byway Scenic Drive. Offers freshwater pond and inland bird viewing along a hiking trail at the Eagle's View Golf and Interpretive Centre. The trail crosses over and skirts MacLure's Pond in Murray River. Take Route 4 form Wood Islands or Montague. In Murray River look for signs, near the bridge. Park in lot and walk to centre where the trails start.

7 Murray Head, Beach Point and Murray Harbour

Kings Byway Scenic Drive. Along the shores and cliffs of Cape Bear, Murray Head, Beach Point and Murray Harbour as well as in adjacent wooded areas, a variety of coastal, marshland, and woodland birds can be spotted, including jays, waxwings, thrushes, cormorants, gannets, scoter, Red-breasted Mergansers, gulls and others. Confederation Trail can be walked or cycled from Murray Harbour to Murray River. Proceed east on Route 4 and then Route 18 from Route 1 at Wood Islands.

Bays & Dunes

8 Souris Harbour and Causeway

Kings Byway Scenic Drive. Waterfowl, shorebirds, and other coastal birds can be viewed on the tidal flats, saltmarshes and bay at Souris. Observe from the causeway linking Souris and Souris West. On Route 2 just east of the intersection with Route 306.

⑨ New Harmony Demonstration Woodlot

Kings Byway Scenic Drive. Woodland birds including thrushes, warblers, flycatchers, vireos, sparrows and other birds common in deciduous and coniferous forests. Woodpeckers, hawks and owls may sometimes be seen along the roads and trails in this increasingly popular eco-tourism destination. From Route 305 take Route 335 to Route 303 (the New Harmony Road) and proceed north to the marked parking area.

⑩ East Point

Kings Byway Scenic Drive. This is the Island's foremost coastal birding site especially on windy days during migration. Gannets, scoter, eider, loon, and sometimes phalaropes, murre, razorbills, and Peregrine Falcon are seen here. Turn east of Route 16 at East Point, proceed to the lighthouse. Parking available.

⑪ Priest Pond

Kings Byway Scenic Drive. On the north shore of the Island, Priest Pond offers opportunities for viewing freshwater marsh, coniferous woodland, edge and coastal birds, as well as swallows. On Route 16 just west of the intersection with Route 302. Roadside parking only.

⑫ Mount Stewart Marsh

Kings Byway Scenic Drive. Waterfowl, heron, Northern Harrier, Osprey, Bald Eagles and Swamp Sparrows can be seen on the marsh, part of a complex eco-system at the head of the Hillsborough River, a designated Canadian Heritage River. Follow Confederation Trail, part of the TransCanada Trail system, eastward from Main Street in Mount Stewart. Mount Stewart is located 18 miles east of Charlottetown off Route 2.

Anne's Land

⑬ Tracadie Bay

Near Kings Byway Scenic Drive. This broad bay along the Island's north shore offers excellent coastal and waterfowl birding opportunities. During migration, visit at mid- to high tide for wading shorebirds. Turn off Route 6 towards Tracadie Harbour at Grand Tracadie and proceed to the approaches to the wharf.

14 Covehead Harbour

Blue Heron Scenic Drive. Adjacent saltmarshes host Sharp-tailed Sparrow during the breeding season and migrating shorebirds and waterfowl in spring and autumn. Normally the best place in province to observe Piping Plover without disturbing the birds. Other probable sightings, depending on season, are Common, Caspian, and Arctic Tern, Semipalmated Plovers and Sandpipers, and other shorebirds, Bald Eagle, Osprey, Northern Harrier, and other raptors. Take Route 15 from Charlottetown to the Prince Edward Island National Park then turn right on the Park's Gulf Shore Parkway. Proceed to the saltmarshes and harbour.

15 Orby Head

Blue Heron Scenic Drive. This coastal cliff along the northern shore of the island in the Prince Edward Island National Park offers excellent viewing of coastal birds, including Black Guillemot, scoter, eider, cormorant, gulls and pelagic birds. Located east of Cavendish off the Park's Gulf Shore Parkway, Orby Head is signposted and has a small parking area.

16 Green Gables Pond

Blue Heron Scenic Drive. Waterfowl and marsh bird viewing in the Prince Edward Island National Park. Located in Cavendish near its excellent beaches. Between Route 6 and the Gulf Shore Parkway at Cavendish Golf Course.

17 Malpeque Bay

Blue Heron Scenic Drive. Designated as a wetland area of international importance, Malpeque Bay is a major migration stopover area for thousands of waterfowl and the breeding site for thousands of cormorants. Whimbrel and plover use adjacent hayfields as well as shore areas. There are good viewpoints of the bay with telescopes from Cabot Beach Provincial Park on the northeast side of the bay, off Route 105. Also accessible from Route 104 at Hamilton and from Route 2 in Sherbrooke by taking the Locke Shore Road to the bay.

Sunsets & Seascapes

18 ## Foxley River Demonstration Woodlot

Lady Slipper Scenic Drive. Coniferous and deciduous woodland birds, including creepers, warblers, vireos, thrushes, grouse and hawks can be sighted along forest trails; cormorants often perch on the pilings adjacent to the nearby Foxley River bridge on route 12. To reach the Demonstration Woodlot interpretive trails, turn off Route 12 at Woodbrook and follow signs to the parking area.

20 ## Black Pond

Lady Slipper Scenic Drive. Offers waterfowl viewing, including coastal and marsh birds. The pond is adjacent to the road along Route 14 on the Island's west coast at Pleasant View.

21 ## Miminegash

Lady Slipper Scenic Drive. Saltwater marshes at Miminegash provide opportunities for sighting coastal birds, waterfowl, and marsh birds. Off Route 14 along the Island's west coast about midway between North Cape and West Point.

19 ## North Cape

Lady Slipper Scenic Drive. Coastal as well as woodland birds — scoter, eider, cormorant, Black Guillemot, gulls and pelagic birds — are among the many attractions of this diverse ecosystem at the Island's northwestern tip. Take Route 12 north to the North Cape Lighthouse. Walk to the point or, on the trail, through the woodlands to the south. Limited parking is available.

22 ## West Point's Fairy Trails

Lady Slipper Scenic Drive. Coniferous forest birds, including Boreal Chickadees, sparrows, thrushes, warblers, and owls, can be sighted along the hiking trails of the Cedar Dunes Provincial Park, where camping facilities are also available. There are also wooded swamp, sand dune, and edge habitats to explore here. Watch out for poison ivy. Take road to the Park off Route 14 in West Point.

Common Loon
Gavia immer

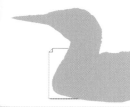

Observation Calendar

J F M A M J J A S O N D

Male/Female: *Summer*: Black head and neck with white banded neck ring; thick grey sharp bill; red eye; white chest and belly; black back and wings spotted white; feet and legs black. *Winter*: Contrasting blacks and whites muted to dark dull brown. In flight: large feet trail behind tail feathers; quick wing beats close to water's surface; takes off from water by running across surface.

Did you know? Loons can remain underwater for more than 5 minutes. They dive to feed and to avoid danger.

Voice: Drawn out *lou-lou-lou-lou* like yodelling, often at dusk or dawn.
Food: Small fish.
Nest/Eggs: Mound built with aquatic plants, mostly on islands. 2 eggs.

Red-throated Loon
Gavia stellata

Beak

Flying

Observation Calendar
J F M A M J J A S O N D

Male/Female: *Winter*: Face changes from grey to white; red throat becomes white; grey speckled head; bill grey; white speckles on black back, white belly. In flight: only loon capable of take off from land; quick wing beats over surface of water.

Voice: When breeding, a variety of high-pitched calls, but quieter than common loon.
Food: Small fish.

Feeding

Horned Grebe
Podiceps auritus

Beak

Flying

Feeding

Observation Calendar

J F M A M J J A S O N D

Male/Female: During breeding season a very bright yellow and orange patch behind bright red eye; bill is short black; gray scaling on back; rust coloured neck and chest; belly white; rump grey. Turns overall grey and white with brilliant red eye in non-breeding season. In flight: white patch on wing.

Voice: Song is various high pitched squeaks and chatters.
Food: Small fish, shrimp, aquatic insects.
Nest/Eggs: Floating platform built of plants and mud anchored to plants. 3-7 eggs.

Pied-billed Grebe

Podilymbus podiceps

Size Identification

Beak

Flying

Observation Calendar

J F M A M J J A S O N D

Male/Female: *Summer*: Overall brown with grey-brown back; yellow eye ring; stout bill, white with distinct black band; black chin; short tail. *Winter*: White ring on bill softens; lighter chin. White tail feathers occasionally revealed when threatened by another bird. In flight: white patch on belly and white trail edge on wings.

Voice: Call is *cow* repeated with *keeech* at end, also various cluckings.
Food: Small fish, amphibians, aquatic insects.
Nest/Eggs: Platform built with aquatic plants in shallow water attached to reeds and other aquatic plants. 5-7 eggs.

Feeding

15   Egg: Actual Size

Northern Gannet

Morus bassanus

Size Identification

Beak

Flying

Feeding

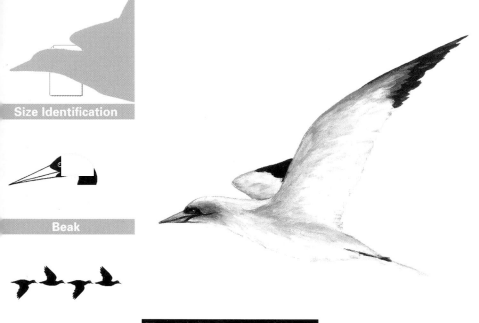

Observation Calendar

J F M A M J J A S O N D

Male/Female: Overall white with black wing tips; pale yellow on side of head; broad grey bill; yellow eye surrounded by black eye ring.

Did you know? When Northern Gannets dive, they fold their wings, becoming like arrowheads. When you see Northern Gannets feeding it is a clue that whales may also be in the area chasing schools of fish.

Voice: Low croaks and grunts, during courtship.
Food: Schooling fish including mackerel and herring.

Great Cormorant

Phalacrocorax carbo

Beak

Flying

Observation Calendar
J F M A M J J A S O N D

Male/Female: Overall black with large grey bill hooked at end; yellow where bill meets the throat, white cheeks and throat; black feet and legs. Larger than Double-crested Cormorant.

Did you know? Cormorants will fly in V-formations in small flocks and are silent in flight.

Feeding

Voice: Variety of grunt-like calls and a croak only at its nest. Elsewhere silent.
Food: Many different types of fish.
Nest/Eggs: Colonies. Platform of sticks lined with seaweed on rocky ledge near water or isolated on an island. 3-4 eggs.

Egg: Actual Size

Double-crested Cormorant

Phalacrocorax auritus

Size Identification

Beak

Flying

Feeding

Male/Female: Overall black with long tail feathers; bright orange chin and throat patch, feet and legs black. Crest is visible only during courtship. In flight: neck is kinked.

Did you know? Cormorants are often seen perched on a rock or pier with wings fully extended to dry their feathers.

Often seen flying extremely high.

Voice: Call is a variety of grunts and croaks, only at its nest. Elsewhere silent.
Food: Small fish.
Nest/Eggs: Colonies. Platform built of sticks and twigs lined with leaves, grass and placed on ground or small tree. 3-5 eggs.

Great Blue Heron

Ardea herodias

Observation Calendar

J F M A M J J A S O N D

Male/Female: Overall grey-blue with black crest on top of head; long neck and bill; black patch connecting eye and long yellow bill; white head; long grey legs and feet; long feathers extend over wings and base of neck. In flight: neck is kinked; legs extend past tail; constant wing flapping with occasional glide.

Voice: Bill makes clacking sound. Call is harsh *squawk*.
Food: Small fish, reptiles, amphibians, crustaceans, birds, aquatic insects.
Nest/Eggs: Colonies. Platform of aquatic plants and twigs lined with softer materials such as down and soft grass, placed in tree. 3-7 eggs.

American Bittern
Botaurus lentiginosus

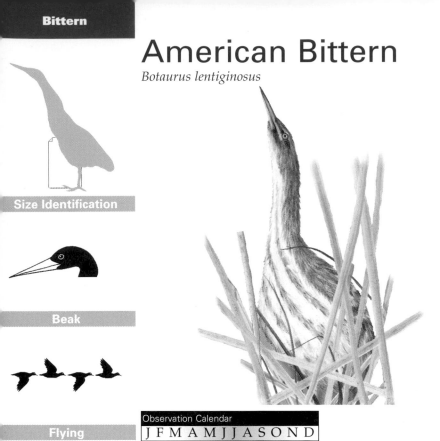

Size Identification

Beak

Flying

Feeding

Egg: Actual Size

Observation Calendar
J F M A M J J A S O N D

Male/Female: Overall reddish brown with white stripes on underside; yellow bill long and sharp; short brown tail lightly banded; smudgy brown back. In flight: tips of wings dark brown.

Did you know? The American Bittern is extremely difficult to spot in the field because, if approached, it will freeze and blend into the reeds.

Voice: In flight, a loud *squark*. Song is a loud *kong-chu-chunk*, on breeding grounds.
Food: Small fish, reptiles, amphibians, insects, small mammals.
Nest/Eggs: Concealed platform built from aquatic plants just above water. 2-6 eggs.

20

Canada Goose
Branta canadensis

Beak

Flying

J F M A M J J A S O N D

Male/Female: Black head, neck and bill; white cheek patch; breast and belly pale brown with white flecks; feet and legs black; back and wings brown with white edging; short black tail; white rump, seen in flight. In flight: flies in "V" formations.

Voice: Musical *honk*, repeated. Female slightly higher pitch *honk*.

Food: Grass, various seed, sand, grain.

Nest/Eggs: Large nest of twigs, moss and grass lined with down feathers placed near water's edge. 4-8 eggs.

Feeding

Egg: 75%

Brant

Branta bernicla

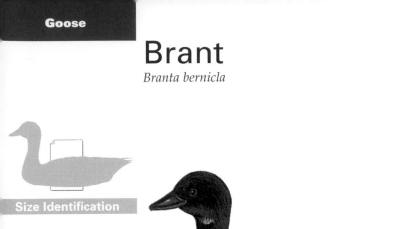

Observation Calendar

J F M A M J J A S O N D

Male/Female: Smaller than Canada Goose with black bill, head, neck and chest; banding of white set against black and gray wings and back; small white patch on neck; belly grey; white rump; feet charcoal grey. In flight: Slightly more irregular "V" formations than Canada Goose; white tail feathers with black edges.

Voice: Soft gargling *rrruk* or *cronk* with a slightly harder sound in flight.
Food: Aquatic plants, grasses, eelgrass.
Nest/Eggs: Semicolonial. Built of seaweeds and grasses and filled with down. Found along rivers and at pond edges. 3-5 eggs

Mallard
Anas platyrhynchos

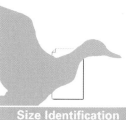

Beak

Observation Calendar
J F M A M J J A S O N D

Flying

Male: Bright green iridescent head, yellow bill; thin white collar; chestnut brown chest; grey sides; black and grey back; white tail; black curled feathers over rump; feet and legs orange. In flight: blue speculum with white border, underparts of wings grey and brown.
Female: Overall brown streaked with orange bill, black patches on bill; white tail feathers.

Feeding

Voice: Male — call soft *raeb* repeated. Female — loud *quacks* repeated.
Food: Aquatic plants, grain, insects.
Nest/Eggs: Shallow cup built of grasses and aquatic plants lined with feathers on ground concealed near water. 8-10 eggs.

23 Egg: Actual Size

American Black Duck
Anas rubripes

Size Identification

Beak

Flying

J F M A M J J A S O N D

Male: Dark black with hint of brown overall and blue speculum; bill is olive; feet and legs orange. In flight: white patches under wings.
Female: Overall lighter brown than male with orange and black bill.

Voice: Both female and male *quack*. Male also whistles.
Food: Vegetation, insects, amphibians, snails, seed, grain, berries.
Nest/Eggs: Depression on ground lined with grass, leaves and down, close to water's edge. 8-12 eggs.

Feeding

Northern Pintail

Anas acuta

Beak

Flying

Feeding

Egg: 90%

Observation Calendar
J F M A M J J A S O N D

Male: Brown head with white line circling around cheeks to chest; white chest and belly; back and wings are black and grey; long tail is black and brown; rump black; sides grey with thin black banding; bill grey with white line. In flight: long tail; white neck and line running up neck.
Female: Overall brown with black bill; no pintail feature.

Voice: Male has 2 high-pitched whistles. Female quacks.
Food: Aquatic plants, seeds, crustaceans, corn, grains.
Nest/Eggs: Bowl of sticks, twigs, grasses and lined with down at a distance from water's edge. 6-9 eggs.

Green-winged Teal
Anas crecca

Size Identification

Beak

Flying

J F M A M J J A S O N D

Male: Head is rust with green patch running around eye to back of head, bill black, black at back of base of neck; warm grey body with thin black banding; distinctive white bar running down side just in front of wing; white rump; short square tail.
Female: Overall dull brown with green speculum; dark band running through eye.

Feeding

Voice: Male — high pitched whistle. Female — weak shrill voice.
Food: Seeds, aquatic plants, corn, wheat, oats.
Nest/Eggs: On ground, cup shaped, filled with grasses and weeds, sometimes a distance from water. 10-12 eggs.

Egg: Actual Size   26

Blue-winged Teal

Anas discors

Beak

Flying

J F M A M J J A S O N D

Male: Grey head with crescent shaped white patch running up face, bill black; chest and belly brown; back and wings dark brown with buff highlights; blue and green speculum; feet and legs yellow.
Female: Overall brown speckled with pale blue speculum.

Voice: Male has high pitched *peeeep*. Female — *quack* is soft high-pitch.
Food: Aquatic plants, seeds.
Nest/Eggs: Pile of grasses lined with down, close to waters edge, concealed. 9-12 eggs.

Feeding

27

American Wigeon
Anas americana

Observation Calendar

J F M A M J J A S O N D

Male: White patch running up forehead from bill; green around eye broadening at cheeks and descending on neck; brown changing to black on back and extremely pointed wings; pointed tail feathers are black, lines with white; bill white with black patches on top and on tip. In flight: green on trailing edge of wing; white forewing and belly.
Female: Overall light brown with brighter colour running down sides. No green patch on eye.

Did you know? The American Wigeon is an opportunist: waiting for other diving ducks to come to the surface with their catch, they will attempt to steal the food.

Voice: Male — occasional distinctive whistle *wh-wh-whew*. Female quacks.
Food: Aquatic plants.
Nest/Eggs: Grasses lined with down, concealed under brush or tree, a distance from water. 9-12 eggs.

Wood Duck
Aix sponsa

Observation Calendar
J F M A M J J A S O N D

Male: Green head and drooping crest; black cheeks; red eye and white throat with two spurs; bill orange with black markings; chest brown with white spots leading to white belly; black and green back; sides tan with white and black band. In flight: long squared tail.

Female: Back and crown brown; white eye ring; speckled breast and lighter coloured belly.

Voice: Male — high-pitch whistle. Female — loud *ooooeeek* in flight.

Food: Aquatic plants, insects, minnows, amphibians.

Nest/Eggs: In cavity of tree, as high as 20 metres, or in a log or built structure lined with wood chips and feathers. 9-12 eggs.

29

Ring-necked Duck
Aythya collaris

J F M A M J J A S O N D

Male: Back, head and breast black, high forehead; black bill with white outlines; yellow eyes; white spur on breast leading to grey underside and belly. In flight: grey speculum; white belly.

Female: Grey cheeks and bill; one white band at tip of bill; white eye ring; dark charcoal back; brown chest, belly and sides.

Voice: Male has low, loud whistle. Female call is soft *prrrrrrrrr* notes. Mostly quiet.

Food: Aquatic plants, molluscs, insects.

Nest/Eggs: Cup-shaped, built of grasses and moss and lined with down feathers, concealed near pond. 8-12 eggs.

Greater Scaup
Aythya marila

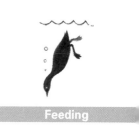

Size Identification

Beak

Flying

Feeding

J F M A M J J A S O N D

Male: *Winter*: Dark green iridescent head neck and chest; white sides and belly; large flat grey bill; yellow eye; grey back with thin black banding; stubby black tail; black feet and legs. *Summer*: Sides and belly brown; head, neck and chest dull brown-black. In flight: large white patches on inside of wings.
Female: Overall dark brown with white face patch. Head held lower than male. In flight: large white patches on trailing edge of wings.

Voice: Male — repeated *waaahooo*. Female — growling *arrrr*. Mostly quiet.
Food: Aquatic plants, crustaceans, molluscs, snails.
Nest/Eggs: Cup-shaped clump of grasses and aquatic plants on ground, lined with down. Often builds on islands. 8-12 eggs.

31

Common Goldeneye
Bucephala clangula

Size Identification

Beak

Flying

Feeding

Observation Calendar

J F M A M J J A S O N D

Male: Black/green head with round white patch on cheek, close to black bill; back black with white bars; underside white; orange feet and legs. In flight: large white speculum.
Female: Brown head and light charcoal overall; bill black with yellow patch; white patches on back. Both male and female are stocky with large head.

Voice: Call during courtship *jeeeeent*. Wings whistle when in flight. Female — low grating sound in flight.
Food: Molluscs, crustaceans, aquatic insects.
Nest/Eggs: In tree cavity or built structure lined with down. 8-12 eggs.

Bufflehead

Bucephala albeola

Size Identification

Beak

Flying

J F M A M J J A S O N D

Male: Small compact duck; black head with large white patch behind the eye, grey bill; black back with white underparts.
Female: Grey-brown overall with smaller white patch behind the eye.

Voice: Mostly quiet. Male whistles. Female quacks.
Food: Small fish, crustaceans, molluscs and snails.

Feeding

Long-tailed Duck

Clangula hyemalis

Size Identification

Beak

Flying

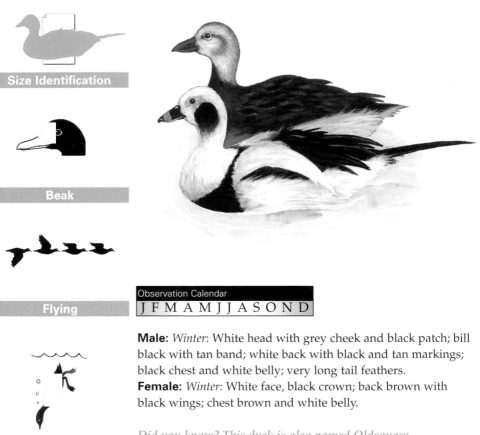

Feeding

Male: *Winter*: White head with grey cheek and black patch; bill black with tan band; white back with black and tan markings; black chest and white belly; very long tail feathers.
Female: *Winter*: White face, black crown; back brown with black wings; chest brown and white belly.

Did you know? This duck is also named Oldsquaw.

Voice: Male — call during courtship sounds similar to yodelling. Female — soft grunting and quacking.
Food: Insect larvae, molluscs, crustaceans.

Common Eider
Somateria mollissima

Observation Calendar

J F M A M J J A S O N D

Male: Large black patch on crown; white face; pale grey-green on back of head and from crown to beak. Overall white with black tail, belly and sides. In flight: wing feathers black.
Female: Overall speckled brown with dark brown on head; bill grey; tail feathers often cocked.

Voice: Male *coooos* during courtship. Female — deep hoarse-sounding *quack*.
Food: Sea urchins, molluscs, crustaceans.
Nest/Eggs: Built of aquatic plants, moss and grasses lined with down feathers placed on ground, preferably rocky terrain. 3-5 eggs.

Egg: 90%

White-winged Scoter
Melanitta fusca

Size Identification

Beak

Flying

Feeding

Observation Calendar
J F M A M J J A S O N D

Male: Black overall with yellow eye and white tear-shaped mark around eye; bill is orange, yellow and white; orange feet and legs. In flight: white wing patch.
Female: Brown overall; white oval on face; white patches on wings.

Voice: Female — low whistle. Male — in courtship is similar to ring of bell.
Food: Clams, scallops, mussels.

Surf Scoter
Melanitta perspicillata

Size Identification

Beak

Flying

J F M A M J J A S O N D

Male: Overall black with white patches on forehead and back of neck; yellow eye; distinctive large orange and red bill with black and white patches on sides.
Female: Overall dark brown with large black bill and vertical white patch behind it; top of head is slightly darker. In flight: pale grey belly.

Did you know? Easy spotting on the Surf Scoter is to look for birds diving directly into the breaking surf hunting for molluscs or crustaceans.

Feeding

Voice: Male — low whistle during courtship.
Food: Mussels, crustaceans, insects, aquatic plants.

37

Black Scoter
Melanitta nigra

Observation Calendar
J F M A M J J A S O N D

Male: Overall black with long thin tail feathers; large yellow knob on top of black bill; feet and legs dark orange.
Female: Overall dark grey with lighter grey on cheeks.

Voice: Low whistle during courtship. Quiet.
Food: Aquatic plants, molluscs, mussels, limpets.

Common Merganser
Mergus merganser

Observation Calendar
J F M A M J J A S O N D

Male: Dark green head crested with red toothed bill slightly hooked at end; white ring around neck connects to white chest and belly; black back and white sides; feet and legs orange.
Female: Brown head and grey-brown back; white chin.

Voice: Male call is *twaang*. Female call is series of hard notes.
Food: Small fish, crustaceans and molluscs.
Nest/Eggs: Built of reeds and grass and lined with down feathers in tree cavity, rock crevice, on ground or in built structure. 8-11 eggs.

Egg: Actual Size

Red-breasted Merganser
Mergus serrator

Beak

Flying

Feeding

Observation Calendar

J F M A M J J A S O N D

Male: *Winter*: Dark green and black head with crest, red eye, white neck ring, long orange toothed bill with slight hook at end; chest white, spotted black; back black with white patching. *Summer*: Head chestnut brown; overall body grey. In flight: rapid wing beats; straight flying pattern. Dark breast on male.
Female: Brown head with grey upper parts and white belly.

Voice: Call for male is *eoooow* usually during courtship. Female — series of hard notes. Mostly quiet.
Food: Small fish, molluscs, crustaceans.
Nest/Eggs: Built of grass and down in sheltered area under bush. 8-10 eggs.

Hooded Merganser
Lophodytes cucullatus

Beak:

Flying

J F M A M J J A S O N D

Male: Black crested head with large white patch on back of head behind eye; black bill is long and thin; rust eye; black back with rust sides and white underparts; black band runs down side into chest; white bands on black wings; tail is often cocked. In flight: rapid energetic wing beats.
Female: Grey breast and belly; faint rust on back of crest; wings dark brown.

Voice: Call is low croaking or *gack*.
Food: Small fish, reptiles, crustaceans, molluscs, and aquatic insects.
Nest/Eggs: In tree cavity or built structure lined with grasses and down feathers, occasionally on ground. 9-12 eggs.

Feeding

41
Egg: Actual Size

Sharp-shinned Hawk
Accipiter striatus

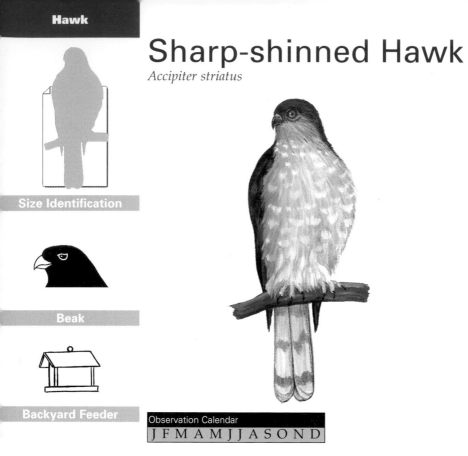

Size Identification

Beak

Backyard Feeder

Observation Calendar
J F M A M J J A S O N D

Male/Female: In flight: small hawk with rust chest banded with buff; long square tail is white with charcoal banding; wings dark brown and rounded; top of head dark brown. Perched: brick-red eyes with brown band just below eye; bill is black with yellow base; feet and legs yellow; white feathers extend out of rust coloured belly.

Did you know? Over the past few years there has been a dramatic decrease in the eastern population. This may be directly related to the decrease in songbirds that it hunts.

Nesting Location

Voice: A quick high pitched *kik kik kik*.
Food: Small songbirds.
Nest/Eggs: Broad platforms of twigs and sticks in conifers or deciduous trees built against the trunk, lined with bark. 4-5 eggs.

Bald Eagle

Haliaeetus leucocephalus

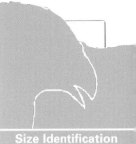

Beak

Observation Calendar

J F M A M J J A S O N D

Male/Female: In flight: broad black wings and belly with white head and tail feathers. Perched: white head with brilliant yellow eyes, white tail feathers, black back and wings, feet and legs yellow; bill yellow.

Juvenile: Mistaken for Golden Eagle because it lacks white head and tail; chest, white and speckled; black wings with white speckles; underparts black with large areas of white.

Did you know? The eagle population is now recovering from rapid declines in the 1970s due to the widespread use of DDT and other insecticides.

Nesting Location

Voice: A loud scream given in multiples.

Food: A variety of small and medium-sized mammals, fish and carrion.

Nest/eggs: Upper parts of large, often dead, trees built with large twigs, lined with grass, moss, sod and weeds. 2 eggs.

Egg: 75%

Northern Harrier (Marsh Hawk)

Circus cyaneus

Size Identification

Beak

J F M A M J J A S O N D

Male: In flight: white underside with black and rust speckles; head is grey; black on tips of wings; orange feet; wings are V-shaped in flight. Perched: grey head with white face mask; yellow eyes; thin rust banding down front; white rump.
Female: Slightly larger than male with brown overall and white rump; buff face disk around cheeks; buff under chin and belly is banded with brown; bill grey; yellow eyes.

Did you know? While gliding over meadows, the Northern Harrier's wings take a V-shape, making it easy to identify.

Nesting Location

Voice: Relatively quiet bird with occasional screams of alarm.
Food: A variety of small mammals and birds.
Nest/Eggs: On or near ground, built of sticks, straw and grasses. 4-5 eggs.

Egg: 90%

44

Osprey
Pandion haliaetus

Size Identification

Beak

Observation Calendar
J F M A M J J A S O N D

Male/Female: In flight: white belly and chest; wings grey with black banding; white wing underparts connect to chest; black band running through eye; large black bill; tail grey with black banding. Perched: black back and wings with thin white line running above wing; eye yellow with black band running through and down to cheek; chin white; top of head white with black patches.
Female: Larger with a pronounced dark necklace.

Voice: A loud chirp which trails off or ascending *squeeeee* during courtship displays.
Food: Various small fish.
Nest/Eggs: Constructed of twigs and sticks, lined with sod, grass and vines in upper parts of trees and on top of poles, 60 feet above ground 2-3 eggs.

Nesting Location

Egg: 70%

45

American Kestrel
Falco sparverius

Size Identification

Beak

Birdhouse Nester

Male/Female: In flight: overall buff with black speckles; distinctive black banding on face. Perched: charcoal wings with black, separated banding; back rust with black banding; grey top of head with rust patch on top; black bands running down cheeks against white; bill black/charcoal with yellow at base; feet and legs orange; tail deep rust with broad black tip.

Voice: Rapid *klee klee klee* or *kily kily kily.*
Food: Mice, voles, insects and small birds.
Nest/Eggs: In cavity of tree or man-made boxes, little or no nesting material. 3-5 eggs.

Nesting Location

Egg: Actual Size   46

Ruffed Grouse

Bonasa umbellus

Size Identification

Beak

Observation Calendar

J F M A M J J A S O N D

Male: Distinctive crest on head; overall brown speckled bird with black shoulder band on back of neck; tail is grey with broad black band at tip; eye brown; feet and legs grey.
Female: Similar to male except browner and more barring on underside; black shoulder band is narrower.

Did you know? The female will act injured if there is a threat near the nest.

Voice: An alarm note of *qit qit*. Cooing by female.
Food: A variety of insects, seeds, tree buds, leaves and berries.
Nest/Eggs: Hollow under log or near the base of a tree lined with leaves, pine needles and feathers. 9-12 eggs.

Nesting Location

47   Egg: Actual Size

Gray Partridge
Perdix perdix

Size Identification

Beak

Observation Calendar
J F M A M J J A S O N D

Male/Female: Overall grey with brick red face and throat, reddish brown banding on wings, feet and legs yellow; bill pale yellow. In flight: brick red tail feathers are exposed.

Did you know? These game birds were introduced to North America from Europe.

Voice: Call is a *keee ukk.*
Food: A variety of seeds, grain, leaves and insects.
Nest/Eggs: Hollow in ground, in thick wooded areas, under felled log or rock, lined with leaves, pine needles and feathers. 9-12 eggs.

Nesting Location

Egg: Actual Size   48

Ring-necked Pheasant
Phasianus colchicus

Beak

J F M A M J J A S O N D

Male: Green iridescent head with distinctive red wattles (patches around eye), white collar, overall body is mixture of grey, black and brown; long tail feathers brown with black banding; feet and legs charcoal grey; pale yellow bill.
Female: Grey-brown overall with dark markers over entire body; pale yellow bill; small red wattle above eye.

Did you know? This chicken-like bird gets into some real cock fights in early spring, jumping, pecking, clawing for their right to territory.

Voice: Similar to a wild turkey gobble at a higher pitch.
Food: Seeds, insects, grains and berries.
Nest/Eggs: Shallow bowl on ground lined with weed, grass and leaves. 6-15 eggs.

Nesting Location

Egg: 80%

Sora

Porzana carolina

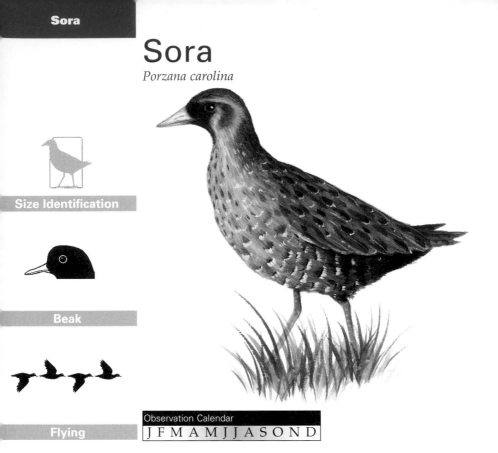

Size Identification

Beak

Flying

J F M A M J J A S O N D

Male/Female: Chicken-like; grey above eye runs down to chin, breast and belly; black mask behind thick yellow bill; upper parts chestnut brown with white and dark brown bars; legs and feet yellow; buff rump.

Did you know? The Sora, like other rails, prefers to migrate at night.

Feeding

Voice: Call is musical *kuur weeee* which is repeated and descends.
Food: Aquatic insects and seeds.
Nest/Eggs: Built in open marsh, attached to reeds, using leaves and grass. 6-15 eggs.

Semipalmated Plover
Charadrius semipalmatus

Size Identification

Beak

Flying

J F M A M J J A S O N D

Male/Female: *Summer*: Dark brown head, back and wings; small white patch on forehead with black band above; faint white eyebrow; white chin extending into white collar with black collar band below; chest and belly white; wing feathers black; feet and legs orange; bill is orange tipped in black. In flight: quick wingbeats with slight glide just before landing.

Voice: Whistle *chee-weee* with a defensive call in quick short notes. Also soft rattling.
Food: Marine worms.

Feeding

Piping Plover
Charadrius melodus

Size Identification

Beak

Flying

Observation Calendar

Observation Calendar

J F M A M J J A S O N D

Male/Female: *Spring and Summer*: Light greyish upperparts with distinctive black band across forehead; bill yellow with black tip; black collar; white chin, cheeks, chest and belly; black wing feathers; feet and legs yellow.
Winter: Black collar band becomes grey; bill black.
In flight: quick wingbeats with slight glide just before landing; white at base of tail and black tail feathers.

Did you know? The Piping Plover is an endangered species and its nesting grounds are under special protection.

Voice: Call is soft whistled *peeeep*.
Food: Insect larvae, molluscs, crustaceans, fly larvae and marine worms.
Nest/Eggs: Scraped out hollow on sand with a few pebbles or shells. 3-4 eggs.

Feeding

Killdeer

Charadrius vociferus

Size Identification

Beak

Flying

J F M A M J J A S O N D

Male/Female: Bright red eye with black band running across forehead; white chin, collar and eyebrow; black collar ring under white; black chest band set against white chest and belly; back and wing rust and grey; wing tipped in black; legs and feet pink/grey. In flight: orange rump; black wing tips and white band on trailing edge.

Did you know? A killdeer will exhibit a "broken-wing" display when a predator comes close to the nest sight. The bird will appear hurt and run around distracting the predator from the nest.

Feeding

Voice: Variety of calls with most common being *kill deeee* which is repeated.
Food: Insects.
Nest/Eggs: Hollow on ground with some pebbles. Most popular sightings in gravel parking lots. 3-4 eggs.

Egg: Actual Size

Black-bellied Plover

Pluvialis squatarola

Size Identification

Beak

Flying

Feeding

Observation Calendar

J F M A M J J A S O N D

Male/Female: *Summer*: Black mask set against pale grey speckled head, crown and neck; bill black; breast and belly black; wings and tail black with white speckles; white rump; feet and legs black. *Winter*: Black face patch; dull grey-brown chest and belly. In flight: black on inner wings underparts; white wing band; white rump.

Voice: Call is whistled 3-note *pee oo ee*.
Food: Marine worms, insects, crustaceans, molluscs, seeds.

Ruddy Turnstone

Arenaria interpres

Size Identification

Beak

Flying

J F M A M J J A S O N D

Male/Female: *Winter*: Speckled brown back, head and wings; white belly, brown bib and white patch on either side; feet and legs dark orange. *Summer*: Overall upperparts brown and black; brown and black bill with white patch just behind bill; black bib with white patch; short black tail. In flight: white bands on wings and back.

Did you know? The Ruddy Turnstone got its name because of its feeding habits. The bird wanders down the feeding area turning over stones.

Feeding

Voice: Call is *tuc e tuc*.
Food: Insects, molluscs, crustaceans, marine worms.

American Woodcock

Scolopax minor

Size Identification

Beak

Male/Female: Distinctive long, straight, narrow bill of light brown; large brown eyes set back on the head; overall brown-black back with buff underside; feet and legs pale pink. In flight: short wings explode with clatter.

Did you know? When courtship is taking place, the males will rise up in the air and circle around as high as 80 metres.

Nesting Location

Voice: A deep *peeeeint* and a tin whistle sounding twitter when in flight.

Food: Earthworms, a variety of insects and insect larvae and seeds.

Nest/Eggs: Shallow depression on ground lined with dead leaves and needles, in wooded area. 4 eggs.

Egg: Actual Size 56

Common Snipe

Gallinago gallinago

Beak

Flying

Observation Calendar
J F M A M J J A S O N D

Male/Female: Very long narrow bill; with small head and large brown/black eye; buff eye ring; black and white bars on white belly; brown back striped with pale yellow; short yellow feet and legs; tail has rust band. In flight: pointed wings; flies in back and forth motion with quick wingbeats.

Did you know? The Common Snipe uses its long bill to hunt in bog-like conditions where it can penetrate through the soft ground to catch prey below the surface.

Feeding

Voice: Call is a *swheet swheet* with sharp *scaip* call when flushed.
Food: Larvae, crayfish, molluscs, insects, frogs and seeds.
Nest/Eggs: Hollow in marsh area, concealed with grass, leaves, twigs and moss. 4 eggs.

Egg: Actual Size

Size Identification

Beak

Flying

Feeding

Whimbrel
Numenius phaeopus

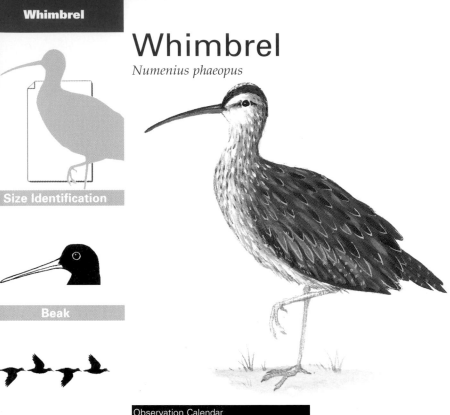

Observation Calendar

J F M A M J J A S O N D

Male/Female: Overall grey and brown speckled with cream sides banded with dark brown; long downward curving black bill with yellow underside; cream eyebrow extending from bill; dark brown cap; feet and legs grey; tail brown with dark brown banding.

Voice: Inflight call is rapid *qui* repeated numerous times with no change in pitch.
Food: Insects, marine worms, crustaceans, mollusks, crabs, berries.
Nest/Eggs: Depression lined with lichens or sedge leaves. 4 eggs.

Spotted Sandpiper
Actitis macularia

Size Identification

Beak

Flying

Male/Female: *Summer*: Grey-brown on head, back and wings; white eyebrow and black line running from beak to back of neck; long orange bill; white chin, chest and belly with distinct charcoal spots; yellow feet and legs; bobbing tail.
Winter: White underparts — no spots. In flight: quick stiff wingbeats, slightly arched back.

Voice: Quiet bird but makes a *peeetaawet* call during courtship and a whistle that is repeated when alarmed.
Food: Insects, worms, crustaceans, fish, flies and beetles.
Nest/Eggs: Shallow depression on ground lined with grasses and mosses. 4 eggs.

Feeding

59

Egg: Actual Size

Willet

Catoptrophorus semipalmatus

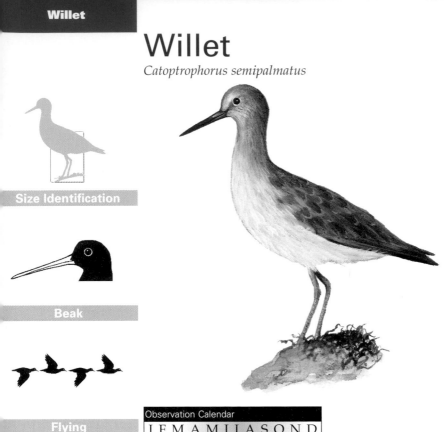

Size Identification

Beak

Flying

Observation Calendar

J F M A M J J A S O N D

Male/Female: Brownish grey and white speckled; white at lower belly and rump; bill is long, heavy greyish yellow; feet and legs grey; black tip on wings.
In flight: distinctive bold white wing band on black tipped wings.

Feeding

Voice: Call is ring-like similar to name *pill will willet* with quieter call *kip* repeated 3-6 times.
Food: Insects, crustaceans, molluscs, grasses and seeds.
Nest/Eggs: On open ground, lined with grasses or bits of shell, a distance from water. 4 eggs.

Greater Yellowlegs

Tringa melanoleuca

Beak

Flying

Observation Calendar

J F M A M J J A S O N D

Male/Female: Speckled grey and white overall; long bright yellow legs and feet; long straight black bill; short tail feathers with black banding; white belly.

Voice: Call is whistled musical *whew* repeated and descending.
Food: Fish, snails, insects, plants.
Nest/Eggs: Hollow on ground in damp area. 4 eggs.

Feeding

Egg: Actual Size

Lesser Yellowlegs

Tringa flavipes

Size Identification

Beak

Flying

Observation Calendar

J F M A M J J A S O N D

Male/Female: Long black bill; dark upperparts speckled white; white belly; wings and tail feathers banded black; long yellow legs and feet.

Voice: Call is *tu* repeated.
Food: Insects, worms, snails, berries, small fish.

Feeding

Red Knot

Calidris canutus

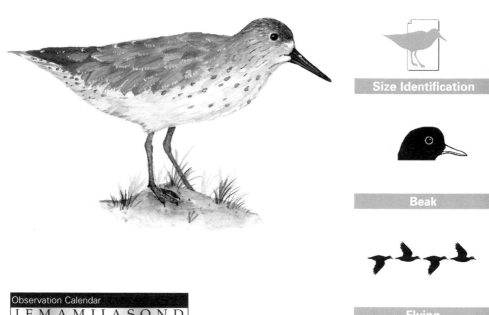

Observation Calendar

J F M A M J J A S O N D

Male/Female: *Winter*: Face, neck and chest turn from brick red in summer to light grey; wings and tail turn dark; black bill; legs and feet charcoal.

Did you know? Red Knots are mostly seen flying in flocks of hundreds of birds with Dunlins, plovers, Godwits, sandpipers and many other shorebirds in their migration journeys.

Feeding

Voice: Call is low *nuuuut*. Soft *currret* in flight.
Food: Molluscs, worms, insects, crabs, seeds.

Pectoral Sandpiper

Calidris melanotos

Size Identification

Beak

Flying

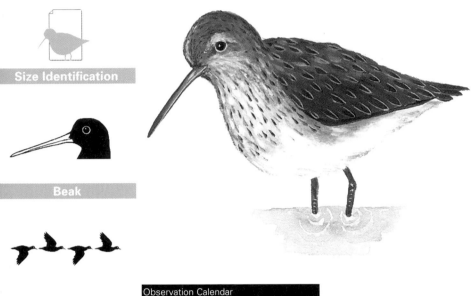

Observation Calendar
J F M A M J J A S O N D

Male/Female: Overall black and brown spotted; bill slightly curved downward, yellow at base and black at tip; small white patch under bill; white eyebrow; black streaked chest; white belly and rump; feet and legs yellow; tail feathers brown and black. In flight: white underwings.

Feeding

Voice: Inflight call is low hard sounding *druuuup* or *churk*.
Food: Insects, grass seeds, worms, crabs.
Nest/Eggs: Substantial nest of grass and leaves in tussock. 4 eggs.

Egg: Actual Size   64

Least Sandpiper

Calidris minutilla

Size Identification

Beak

Flying

J F M A M J J A S O N D

Male/Female: Long downward curved black bill; overall brown and black; belly and rump white; feet and legs are yellow Overall colour turns grey in non-breeding seasons. In flight: v-shaped wings white on undersides.

Voice: High pitched *kreeeep* rising up. When in flock it gives high repeated notes.
Food: Insects, mollusks, crustaceans and marine worms.
Nest/Eggs: Shallow depression on bog or upland. 4 eggs.

Feeding

65

Egg: Actual Size

Semipalmated Sandpiper

Calidris pusillus

Size Identification

Beak

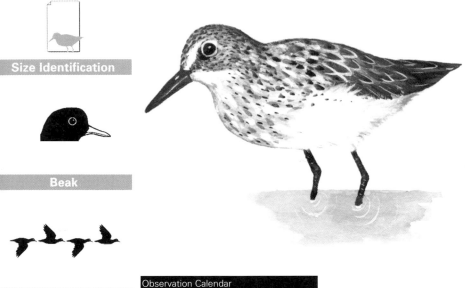

Flying

Observation Calendar
J F M A M J J A S O N D

Male/Female: Short, straight black bill; back is grey-brown; white underparts; black legs with slightly webbed front toes. In winter, uniformly grey on back. In flight: distinctive formations of thousands of birds stretching hundreds of metres, showing white underparts in unison.

Feeding

Voice: Continuous quavering *churrrk*.
Food: Small marine invertebrates usually on mud flats.
Nest/Eggs: Depression lined with grass and leaves on margins of fresh and salt water. 4 eggs.

Sanderling

Calidris alba

Beak

Flying

J F M A M J J A S O N D

Male/Female: *Summer*: Bright brown and speckled on head, back and breast; black tail; white belly; long bill is dark brown; feet and legs black. *Winter*: Light grey head, neck and chest; white cheeks, white belly; tail black. In flight: white on underwing; white bar on top side of wing.

Voice: Call is *kip* in flight. Chattering during feeding.
Food: Crustaceans, molluscs, marine worms, insects.

Feeding

Short-billed Dowitcher

Limnodromus griseus

Size Identification

Beak

Flying

Feeding

Observation Calendar

J F M A M J J A S O N D

Male/Female: *Summer*: Rust neck and chest speckled black; back and wings dark brown speckled with buff; dark brown cap on head. *Winter*: Grey speckled overall with dark, barred flanks; black bill fading to yellow near base, white eyebrows; black and brown tail feathers; feet and legs yellow.

Voice: Call is *tu*, repeated several times in soft high-pitch.
Food: Marine worms, molluscs, insects.

Red-necked Phalarope

Phalaropus lobatus

Size Identification

Beak

Flying

Feeding

Observation Calendar

J F M A M J J A S O N D

Male/Female: *Winter*: White and grey chest and belly. Face white with black mark behind eye; dark grey wings and back.
Male: *Summer*. Top of head black; long black bill; white chin; black band running under eye against white and rust; rust neck; grey chest changing to white belly; dark brown and rust wings and back; tail black; white rump.
Female: Overall similar markings except bolder colour; and rufous neck with more contrast overall.

Voice: Call is sharp *twic*.
Food: Aquatic insects, molluscs, crustaceans.

Iceland Gull

Larus glaucoides kumlieni

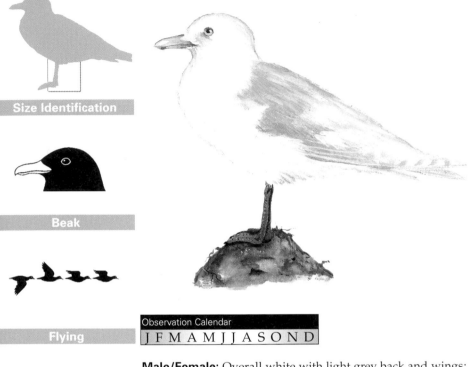

Size Identification

Beak

Flying

Observation Calendar

J F M A M J J A S O N D

Male/Female: Overall white with light grey back and wings; white wings underside; yellow bill with red tip on lower part; yellow eye; dark pink feet and legs. In flight: overall white and grey underparts; white patches on wing tips.

Voice: Mostly quiet. Variety of squeaks.
Food: Fish, carrion, bird eggs.

Feeding

Great Black-backed Gull

Larus marinus

Beak

Flying

Feeding

Observation Calendar

J F M A M J J A S O N D

Male/Female: White head, chin, chest and belly, red patch on lower portion of bill; feet and legs pink/grey; black wings with thin white band on trailing edge; tail and back black. In flight: pale grey undersides with black wing tip; tail white.

Voice: Loud squawks and deep guttural notes.
Food: Scavenger. Small fish, mammals, young birds and garbage. Major predator of other birds including puffin and tern chicks.
Nest/Eggs: Colonies. Mound of seaweed and other coastal plants lined with grasses on ground or rocky ledge. 3 eggs.

71   **Egg: 80%**

Herring Gull
Larus argentatus

Size Identification

Beak

Flying

Feeding

Observation Calendar

J F M A M J J A S O N D

Male/Female: White head that in winter is streaked light brown; yellow eye and bill; small red patch on lower bill; tail black; feet and legs red. In flight: grey wing with white on trailing edge and black tips; pale brown rump; wide charcoal tail feathers.

Voice: Variety of squawks and squeals. Aggressive alarm call is *kak kak kak kak* ending in *yucca*.
Food: Insects, small mammals, clams, fish, small birds, crustaceans, mussels, rodents, garbage.
Nest/Eggs: Colonies. Mound lined with grass and seaweed on ground or cliff. Usually on islands. 2-4 eggs.

Egg: 90%

Ring-billed Gull
Larus delawarensis

Beak

Flying

Observation Calendar
J F M A M J J A S O N D

Male/Female: *Summer*: White overall; yellow bill with black band at end; yellow eye; pale grey wings and black tips and white patches within black tips; black feet and legs. *Winter*: Feet and legs turn yellow; light brown spots on top of head and back of neck. In flight: grey underparts; black wing tips.

Voice: Loud *kaawk* and other calls.
Food: Insects, bird eggs, worms, garbage.
Nest/Eggs: Colonies. Grasses, sticks, twigs and pebbles built on ground. 3 eggs.

Feeding

Egg: Actual Size

Bonaparte's Gull

Larus philadelphia

Size Identification

Beak

Flying

Observation Calendar

J F M A M J J A S O N D

Male/Female: Smaller gull with dark head and bill; white neck, chest and belly; grey back and black tail feathers. During winter months black cap disappears and a small black spot on side of head turns white. In flight: wings appear black tipped.

Voice: Low rasping *gerrrr* or *wreeeek*.
Food: Small fish, worms and ground insects.
Nest/Eggs: Built of sticks and twigs and lined with grasses placed in spruce or fir tree 5-20 feet above ground. 3 eggs.

Feeding

Common Tern
Sterna hirundo

Observation Calendar
J F M A M J J A S O N D

Male/Female: *Summer*: Soft grey overall with black-cap; white cheeks; long thin red bill with black tip; short, red feet and legs; wings and tail feathers grey, exceptionally long, white underside to tail.
Winter: Black cap recedes leaving white face; black bar on wing; charcoal on tail. In flight: charcoal on wing tips; grey overall; quick wingbeats.

Voice: Short *kip* repeated and louder *keeeear.*
Food: Small fish.
Nest/Eggs: Colonies. On ground, cup of grasses on sandy or pebbled areas. Most often on islands. 2-3 eggs.

75

Arctic Tern
Sterna paradisaea

Size Identification

Beak

Flying

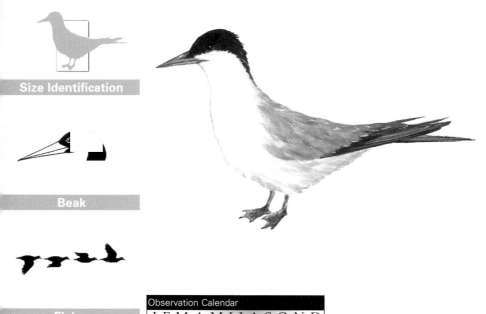

Male/Female: Black head with long sharp red bill; overall grey; exceptionally long thin tail; red feet and legs are very short. In flight: white rump and lower back.

Did you know? Terns have the ability to hover over the surface of the water when hunting for prey.

Feeding

Voice: Loud high-pitched *kee ar* or *kip-kip-kip-kee-ar*.
Food: Small fish.
Nest/Eggs: On ground, lined with grasses and shells, on rocky ledge or beach, often in colonies, isolated from human habitation. 2 eggs.

Caspian Tern
Sterna caspia

Beak

Flying

Male/Female: Largest tern with distinctive black cap; long sharp orange bill; white neck, chest and belly; grey back with long grey wings; short white tail; feet black. Juvenile feet often yellow.

Voice: Deep heronlike *aayayam* and harsh *cahar*.
Food: Small fish.
Nest/Eggs: Mostly nests in colonies. Nest is a depression in ground lined with grass and seaweed on a sandy beach. 2-3 eggs.

Feeding

77   Egg: 85%

Atlantic Puffin
Fratercula artica

Size Identification

Beak

Flying

Observation Calendar

J F M A M J J A S O N D

Male/Female: *Summer*: Only puffin in eastern regions. Large colourful bill with white mask; black collar, head and back; white chest and belly; orange eye ring; wings and tail black; orange feet and legs. *Winter*: Markings slightly duller.

Voice: Hard sounding *urrrr* and croaks.
Food: Small fish, crustaceans and squid.

Feeding

Rock Dove (Pigeon)

Columba livia

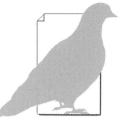

Beak

Backyard Feeder

Observation Calendar
J F M A M J J A S O N D

Male/Female: Varies greatly from solid white to solid black and everything in between. Most birds have dark grey head with hints of iridescent colours along the neck; body light grey with two charcoal wing bands; tail and wings dark grey with black bands; rump is white.

Did you know? Pigeons were introduced to North America in the 1800s. They are now prevalent everywhere, especially in urban areas.

Voice: Soft descending *kooooo kooooo*.
Food: Seeds and grain
Nest/Eggs: Flimsy nest of twigs, grass, straw and debris, on ledges or crevices of buildings and bridges, in colonies. 1-2 eggs.

Nesting Location

Egg: Actual Size

Mourning Dove
Zenaida macroura

Size Identification

Beak

Backyard Feeder

Observation Calendar

J F M A M J J A S O N D

Male: Buff coloured head and body; dark grey wings and tail; bill is black with speckles of red at opening; wings have small black feathers highlighted against softer grey, eyes black surrounded by light blue; feet and legs red; tail is long and pointed.

Female: Similar except for head, neck and chest are evenly brown.

Did you know? When the mourning dove is in flight its wings whistle.

Nesting Location

Voice: Very distinct cooing that sounds a little sad, *coooahooo oo oo oo* fading at the end.

Food: A variety of seeds and grain

Nest/Eggs: Platform of sticks and twigs, lined with grass and rootlets, in evergreens, 15 metres above ground. 1-2 eggs.

Great Horned Owl
Bubo virginianus

Beak

Observation Calendar
J F M A M J J A S O N D

Male/Female: Very recognizable ear tufts that sit wide apart; bright yellow eyes surrounded by rust colour; grey and brown overall with black bands.

Voice: Hoot consists of several *hoo hoo hoo hoo hoo hoo*.
Food: Small mammals, birds and reptiles.
Nest/Eggs: Nests in a deserted hawk's, heron's or crow's nest with very little material added. Occasionally will lay eggs on ground amongst bones, skulls and bits of fur. 1-3 eggs.

Nesting Location

81

Egg: 70%

Snowy Owl

Nyctea scandiaca

Size Identification

Beak

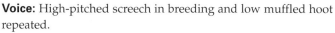
J F M A M J J A S O N D

Male/Female: Short black bill; overall white with brilliant yellow eye; small amount of grey speckling throughout with very faint grey banding on chest and sides; feet are covered in white feathers with long black claws.

Voice: High-pitched screech in breeding and low muffled hoot repeated.
Food: Small mammals, fish, birds and carrion.
Nest/Eggs: Slight depression on ground lined with moss and grass. 3-10 eggs.

Nesting Location

Barred Owl

Strix varia

Size Identification

Beak

Observation Calendar

J F M A M J J A S O N D

Male/Female: Large dark eyes set in buff and rich brown; white bands extend out from face, down the back including wings and tail feathers; chest white with rich brown feathers in columns; bill is small yellow hook shape.

Did you know? The Barred Owls' ears are positioned differently on either side of the head. This allows for better hearing in total darkness.

Voice: Very rhythmic hoots in series of four or five at a time.
Food: Small mammals.
Nest/Eggs: Cavity of tree or abandoned hawk's or crow's nests; no lining added. 2-3 eggs.

Birdhouse Nester

Nesting Location

83

Egg: 60%

Short-eared Owl
Asio flammeus

Size Identification

Beak:

Observation Calendar

J F M A M J J A S O N D

Male/Female: Dark brown overall with buff banding on back; small ear tufts black and buff directly above eyes on top of head (rarely seen); wings and tail feathers dark brown with buff bands; light buff chest and belly with brown streaks; long wings tipped black at the ends; eyes brilliant yellow surrounded by black; bill black; feet and legs black.

Did you know? The Short-eared Owl flies low to the ground when hunting but is able to hover momentarily when prey is spotted.

Nesting Location

Voice: Raspy *yip yip yip.*
Food: Small mammals, mostly voles, songbirds and game birds.
Nest/Eggs: Slight depression hidden in grass. Lined with grass and feathers. 4-9 eggs.

Egg: 65%   84

Northern Saw-whet Owl

Aegolius acadicus

Observation Calendar

J F M A M J J A S O N D

Male/Female: Yellow eyes that are surrounded by a reddish brown facial disk; chest white with brown streaks running length of body; feet and legs grey.

Voice: Whistled song repeated *too too too.*
Food: Diet consists mainly of small mammals, including voles, chipmunks, and bats.
Nest/Eggs: Cavity of dead tree, 4-18 metres above ground. No material added. 2-6 eggs.

Nesting Location

Egg: Actual Size

Ruby-throated Hummingbird

Archilochus colubris

Size Identification

Beak

Backyard Feeder

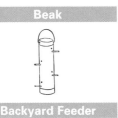

Male: Dark green head which is iridescent in parts; red throat begins darker under chin; white collar, breast and belly; wings and notched tail black; iridescent green on back; black bill is long and thin; small white area behind eyes; feet and legs black.

Female: Head, back and parts of tail are bright iridescent green; white throat, chest and belly; wings and tail black with white outer tips; black bill is long and thin; small white area behind eyes; feet and legs black.

Nesting Location

Voice: A low *hummmmmmm* followed occasionally by a angry sounding squeak or chattering.

Food: Nectar from a variety of plants including thistles, jewelweed, trumpet vines and other blossoms, occasionally insects.

Nest/Eggs: Thimble-size, tightly woven cup with deep cavity built with fibres and attached with spider web, lined with plant down, covered on the outside with lichens, in tree or shrub, 3-6 metres above ground. 2 eggs.

Belted Kingfisher
Ceryle alcyon

Beak

Flying

Observation Calendar
J F M A M J J A S O N D

Male: A large crested blue/black head and long black bill; wings black with white bands; chest white; white collar wraps around neck with blue band that wraps around chest; very short blue tail; feet and legs charcoal.
Female: Rust-coloured breast band.

Did you know? Belted Kingfishers teach their young to dive for food by catching a fish, stunning it, then placing it on the surface of the water. The young birds then practice diving for it.

Feeding

Voice: A continuous deep rattle during flight.
Food: Small fish, amphibians, reptiles, insects and crayfish.
Nest/Eggs: A cavity or tunnel excavated in a bank near a river or lake. 5-8 eggs.

Egg: Actual Size

Yellow-bellied Sapsucker

Sphyrapicus varius

Observation Calendar

J F M A M J J A S O N D

Male: Crown and throat scarlet with black border; white line extending back above eye; black patch on breast; black back marked with white; underbody yellowish white.
Female: Throat white.
In flight: shows conspicuous white wing stripe.

Voice: A high whining *meeewj.*
Food: Sap and insects attracted to sap, berries.
Nest/Eggs: Nests in cavities in dead or dying trees, especially poplars. 3-7 eggs.

Downy Woodpecker
Picoides pubescens

Beak

Backyard Feeder

Birdhouse Nester

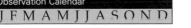
Observation Calendar
J F M A M J J A S O N D

Male: Black crown ends in very bright red spot on back of head; white extends from cheeks to lower belly; wings and tail black with white banding; feet and legs grey.
Female: Similar except without red spot on back of head.

Voice: A bright sounding *peek...peek* which may be followed by a rattling call. Listen for bird pounding on trees looking for insects.
Food: Larvae and other tree-dwelling insects.
Nest/Eggs: Cavity of tree with no added material, 1-5 metres above ground. 3-6 eggs.

Nesting Location

Egg: Actual Size

Eastern Kingbird
Tyrannus tyrannus

Size Identification

Beak

Observation Calendar

J F M A M J J A S O N D

Male/Female: Black head, back, wings and tail; white chin, chest and belly; wings have white along edge and tail has white band along tip; feet and legs black.

Did you know? Size does not matter to the Eastern Kingbird: they will attack crows, ravens, hawks and owls to defend their territory.

Voice: Several different calls including *tzi tzee* as a true song. Also a *kitter kitter kitter* when threatened.

Nesting Location

Food: Flying insects and fruit in late summer.

Nest/Eggs: Bulky cup built with weed stalks, grass and moss, in branches of tree or shrub, 3-6 metres above ground. 3-5 eggs.

Egg: Actual Size   90

Least Flycatcher

Empidonax minimus

Observation Calendar
J F M A M J J A S O N D

Male/Female: Smallest of the flycatchers with a brown/olive head and back; rump is slightly golden; throat white and washes to a grey breast and a pale yellow belly; black eye is ringed with white; wings dark brown and black with white wing bands; tail dark olive/brown with white edges.

Did you know? The Least Flycatcher is not afraid of humans and in pursuit of a flying insect will dive within inches of a person.

Voice: Song is *chibic chibic chibic* repeated with accent in middle of phrase.
Food: Flying insects.
Nest/Eggs: Compact and deep cup built with bark, weeds, grasses and lined with thistle, feathers, hair and fibres, in upright fork of tree or shrub, 1-20 metres above ground. 3-6 eggs.

Eastern Wood-Pewee
Contopus virens

Observation Calendar

J F M A M J J A S O N D

Male/Female: Olive-grey overall with head that is crested at back; wings black and dark grey with two white bars; throat and chest white; belly slightly yellow or white; tail charcoal; bill black on top and yellow underside; feet and legs black.

Did you know? The Wood-Pewee changes its voice in morning and evening, converting its song into a slow verse.

Voice: A soft whistle *pee-a-wee pee-awee* repeated without any pause early in the morning.
Food: Flies, beetles, bees, ants and other insects.
Nest/Eggs: Shallow cup built with grass, spider's web and fibres lined with hair, covered outside with lichens, on horizontal branch of tree far out from trunk, 5-20 metres above ground. 3-5 eggs.

Horned Lark

Eremophila alpestris

Beak

J F M A M J J A S O N D

Male/Female: Dull brown on top; chest and belly white; wings and tail brown and black; distinctive black facial marks which include small horns (feathers) on either side of its head; chin pale yellow with black band above running through eye and down; feet and legs black.

Did you know? The horns are not always visible but a quick way to identify the Horned Lark is that on the ground it walks and does not hop, like most small birds.

Voice: Soft twittering *tsee titi* or *zzeeet*.
Food: A variety of insects, seeds and grains.
Nest/Eggs: Hollow in ground under grass tuft, made of stems and leaves, lined with grass. 3-5 eggs.

Nesting Location

93 Egg: Actual Size

Tree Swallow
Tachycineta bicolor

Beak

Birdhouse Nester

Nesting Location

Observation Calendar

J F M A M J J A S O N D

Male/Female: Dark iridescent blue on head, neck, back, wings and tail; bright white chin, chest and belly; black bill is short and slightly curved; wings are very long reaching down to tip of tail when folded; feet and legs charcoal.

Did you know? The Tree Swallow is the only swallow that eats berries in the place of insects. This allows it to winter further north than its relatives.

Voice: Early morning song *wheet trit weet*, with an alarm call of *cheedeeep*.
Food: Flying insects and berries.
Nest/Eggs: Cup in cavity of tree lined with grass and feathers, usually a woodpecker's old hole. 4-6 eggs.

Bank Swallow

Riparia riparia

Observation Calendar
J F M A M J J A S O N D

Male/Female: Dirty brown overall with white front except for brown band running across chest; wings are very long reaching down to tip of tail when folded; feet and legs grey; black bill is short and curved.

Voice: A variety of calls including *tchirrt tchirrt* and long twittering.

Food: Flying insects as well as a variety of other insects. Main diet consists of dragonflies, flies, mayflies and beetles.

Nest/Eggs: Earth tunnel lined with grass and straw along bank of water. 4-6 eggs.

Barn Swallow
Hirundo rustica

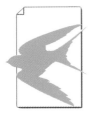

Beak

Observation Calendar
J F M A M J J A S O N D

Male: Dark blue iridescent from top of head, shoulders, down back and top of wings; chin and chest rust colour that fades to white at belly; wings are very long and extend to tips of tail which is forked with long feathers at either end that can be seen when bird is in flight; feet and legs charcoal; black and cream bill. When bird is in flight a band of white can be seen at end of wings.
Female: Same markings but duller.

Did you know? Barn Swallows are amazing to watch as they skim over water and pick insects off the surface. In the evening they hunt mosquitoes.

Nesting Location

Voice: A soft twittering *kvik kvik wit wit*.
Food: A variety of insects.
Nest/Eggs: Mud and straw lined with feathers, in buildings, under bridges, in cliffs and caves. 4-5 eggs.

Egg: Actual Size   96

Blue Jay

Cyanocitta cristata

Beak

Backyard Feeder

J F M A M J J A S O N D

Male/Female: Bright blue crested head with black band running through eye to just under crest on back of neck; black band continues along side of neck on both sides to chest; white under chin; back is blue; wings and tail are blue banded with black and tipped with white at ends; black bill is large with light feathers covering nostril area; feet and legs black.

Did you know? The Blue Jay has a bad reputation for eating eggs of other birds, and even their young.

Voice: Call is *jay jay jay*, plus many other calls including mimicking hawks.

Food: Omnivorous — in summer months the Blue Jay feasts on just about anything, including spiders, snails, salamanders, frogs, seeds and caterpillars. In winter months they supplement their diet with acorns and other nuts stored in tree cavities earlier in the year.

Nest/Eggs: Bulky nest of sticks, leaves, string and moss lined with small roots, well hidden, 1-15 metres above ground, in tree or shrub. 3-4 eggs.

Nesting Location

97 **Egg: Actual Size**

Common Raven
Corvus corax

Beak

Observation Calendar
J F M A M J J A S O N D

Male/Female: Shiny, black bird overall with a blue tint; feet and legs black; black bill is long and wide and has been described as a "Roman nose"; rounded tail.

Voice: Variety of calls including buzzing, croaks and gulps.
Food: A variety of insects, carrion, small mammals and food waste.
Nest/Eggs: Large basket of twigs, sticks, vines, hair and moss, lined with animal hair, on ledge, in tree or shrub. 3-4 eggs.

Nesting Location

Egg: 80%　　98

American Crow

Corvus brachyrhynchos

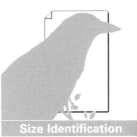

Beak

Backyard Feeder

J F M A M J J A S O N D

Male/Female: Overall shiny black with a hint of purple in direct sunlight; large broad black bill; short and slightly square tail; feet and legs black.

Did you know? Although one might think that crows are a nuisance bird, they actually devour large quantities of grasshoppers, beetles and grubs that can be destructive to crops.

Voice: A variety of calls. Most common is the long *caaaaaw* which softens at the end.
Food: Omnivorous — insects, food waste, grains, seeds and carrion.
Nest/Eggs: Large basket of twigs, sticks, vines, moss, feathers, fur and hair, on ledge in crotch of tree or shrub. 3-4 eggs.

Nesting Location

Egg: Actual Size

Black-capped Chickadee

Poecile atricapilla

Size Identification

Beak

Backyard Feeder

Observation Calendar

J F M A M J J A S O N D

Male/Female: Round black head with white cheeks; black chin that contrasts against bright white bib which fades into rust on belly with buff edges; wings black and grey with white edges; tail black with white edges; feet and legs black.

Did you know? In winter Black-capped Chickadees form small flocks of about 10 birds and defend their territory from intruders.

Voice: A descending whistle with two notes and sounds like *chick-a-dee-dee-dee.*

Food: Seeds, insects and berries. Drawn to thistle-seed feeders.

Nest/Eggs: Domed cup lined with wool, hair, fur, moss and insect cocoons, in cavity of tree. 5-10 eggs.

Nesting Location

Boreal Chickadee

Poecile hudsonica

Birdhouse Nester

Nesting Location

Observation Calendar
J F M A M J J A S O N D

Male/Female: Dirty brown cap with white cheeks; black chin contrasted against white belly with rust colour sides; back brown; wings and tail charcoal with white edges and black tips; feet and legs charcoal.

Did you know? During winter months they will forage for food with Black-capped Chickadees searching for hibernating insects and insect eggs.

Voice: Song is slow *chick che day day day* with calls that are distinctive chip.
Food: Insects, insect eggs, seeds.
Nest/Eggs: Domed nest lined with fur, hair, plant down, moss and feathers in cavity of tree or dug in decaying stump. 4-9 eggs.

Egg: Actual Size

Red-breasted Nuthatch
Sitta canadensis

Size Identification

Beak

Backyard Feeder

Birdhouse Nester

Nesting Location

Observation Calendar
J F M A M J J A S O N D

Male: Small round bird with black stripe over top of head and white stripe underneath running over eye to back of head, followed by another black band running through eye; white cheeks turn to rust at neck and continue rust to chest and belly; back is grey-blue; wings and tail grey becoming black at ends; black bill is often white on underside; feet and legs brown-black.
Female: Similar to male except for grey cap and light underside.

Did you know? The Red-breasted Nuthatch will smear pitch at the entrance to its nest, although it is not known why.

Voice: A tin-whistle call and an occasional loud *knack knack*.
Food: Seeds, insects and flying insects
Nest/Eggs: Cup lined with grass, moss and feathers, in excavated cavity or crevice of tree. 1-12 metres above ground. 4-7 eggs.

Egg: Actual Size

American Robin
Turdus migratorius

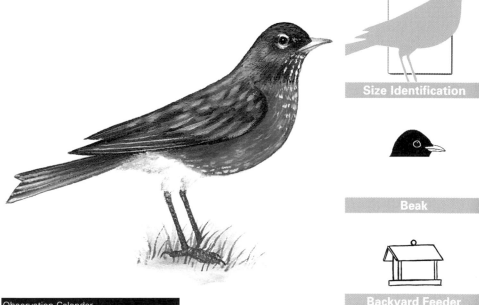

Size Identification

Beak

Backyard Feeder

Male: Charcoal/brown head with distinctive white above and below eye; back and wings charcoal brown with white edges; tail dark grey; neck dark grey with thin white banding; chest and belly brick red; feet and legs black; bill yellow with black at either end.
Female: Breast is slightly paler than male's.

Voice: Song is *cheerily cheerily cheerily* in a whistle tone.
Food: Earthworms, insects and fruit.
Nest/Eggs: Deep cup built with weed stalks, cloth, string and mud, lined with grass, in evergreens and deciduous trees or shrubs. 4 eggs.

Nesting Location

103 **Egg: Actual Size**

Hermit Thrush
Catharus guttatus

Size Identification

Beak

Observation Calendar
J F M A M J J A S O N D

Male/Female: Dusty brown head, neck and back that blends into a rust tail; white eye ring; wings rust when open with black ends; neck and chest white and dark spotted; underparts grey, feet and legs grey with pink; bill black and rust.

Did you know? Not surprisingly, a Hermit Thrush prefers the seclusion of deep wooded areas.

Nesting Location

Voice: Sweet song with a variety of phrases. When disturbed it sounds a *kuk kuk kuk kuk*.

Food: A variety of insects, worms, caterpillars, snails and various fruits.

Nest/Eggs: Bulky ground nest built with twig, bark, grass and moss and lined with conifer needles, fibre and small roots in damp and cool wooded areas. 3-4 eggs.

Swainson's Thrush

Catharus ustulata

Size Identification

Beak

Observation Calendar
J F M A M J J A S O N D

Male/Female: Buff eye-ring and line to base of bill; breast and sides of throat heavily spotted; sides olive brown; ends of wings and tail dark grey; underparts white; legs pink.

Voice: Call like a drop of water — *whoit*; song whip poor will a will e zee zee zee.
Food: Forages the forest floor: insects and a variety of berries.
Nest/Eggs: Twigs, grass and other materials in coniferous trees and shrubs. 3-4 eggs.

Nesting Location

Egg: Actual Size

Golden-crowned Kinglet
Regulus satrapa

Size Identification

Beak

Observation Calendar

J F M A M J J A S O N D

Male: One of the smallest woodland birds with black head stripes that set off its crown patch of orange with yellow edges; neck and back olive-grey; wings and tail black with olive along edges; feet and legs black; pale grey wingbars; pale eyebrow.
Female: Similar to male except patch on top is yellow.

Did you know? Their movements on a tree make them easy to spot. They flutter their wings as they look for insects.

Nesting Location

Voice: Very high pitched dropping to a quick chatter. The song is so highly pitched that some people cannot hear its song.
Food: A variety of insects, spiders, fruits and seeds.
Nest/Eggs: Deep cup built with moss and lichen at top, lined with black rootlets and feathers suspended from conifer branch, up to 30 metres above ground. 5-11 eggs.

Ruby-crowned Kinglet

Regulus calendula

Observation Calendar
J F M A M J J A S O N D

Male: Olive-grey overall with white eye ring broken at top; crested with red patch on head; chin and neck are lighter olive grey, feet and legs black; wings and tail black with white edges; white bands on wings.

Female: Similar to male except for no red patch on top of head.

Did you know? The ruby red top on the male is hard to see except when he is courting when it will flare up.

Voice: High pitched *tee tee tee* followed by a lower *tew tew tew* and ending with a chatter.

Food: Insects, insect eggs, spiders, fruits and seeds.

Nest/Eggs: Deep woven cup built with moss, lichen at top and lined with small black roots and feathers, suspended from conifer branch. 5-10 eggs.

Cedar Waxwing

Bombycilla cedrorum

Size Identification

Beak

Observation Calendar

J F M A M J J A S O N D

Male/Female: Crested brown head with black mask running from black bill, through eyes, to behind head; white outline around mask; back brown; chest and belly yellow-brown; wings black-grey with white edges; wings and tail have red tips; rump white.

Did you know? The name derives from the fact that their wings and tail look as though they have been dipped in red wax.

Nesting Location

Voice: Extremely high pitched *seeee*.
Food: A variety of berries.
Nest/Eggs: Loose woven cup of grass, twigs, cotton fibre and string, lined with small roots, fine grass and down, in open wooded areas in tree or shrub, 2-6 metres above ground. 4-5 eggs.

Egg: Actual Size   108

European Starling

Sturnus vulgaris

Beak

Backyard Feeder

Birdhouse Nester

Nesting Location

Egg: Actual Size

Observation Calendar

J F M A M J J A S O N D

Male/Female: *Summer:* Black iridescent bird in summer with light white speckles over entire body; bill is sharp yellow; wing and tail are edged in white and brown; feet and legs are red. *Winter:* Speckles increase and some become brown; bill is black; feet and legs are red; wings and tail have more brown.

Did you know? Sixty starlings were introduced into New York City in 1890. Since then they have spread throughout North America.

Voice: Mimics the songs of other birds and even sounds of cats and whistles.

Food: A variety of insects including worms and grubs and weed seeds.

Nest/Eggs: Loose cup in cavity filled with grass, leaves, cloth and feathers, up to 18 metres above the ground. 4-5 eggs.

Red-eyed Vireo
Vireo olivaceus

Size Identification

Beak

J F M A M J J A S O N D

Male/Female: *Spring:* red eye encircled with thin line of black set against a wide white eyebrow that runs from bill to back of head; black bill; throat and chest white; feet and legs black; back and rump are olive green; wings and tail black with edges of olive green; eye is darker brown in winter.

Voice: The Red-eyed Vireo may sound over 40 different phrases in just 60 seconds, then begin all over again. A variety of short phrases which includes *cherrrwit chereeee cissy a witt teeeooo.*

Food: Small insects, berries and fruit.

Nest/Eggs: Deep cup built with grass, paper, bark, rootlets, vine and decorated outside with spider's web and lichen, suspended in branches, up to 18 metres above ground; 2 eggs.

Nesting Location

Egg: Actual Size 110

Black-and-white Warbler

Mniotilta varia

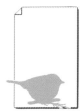

Beak

Observation Calendar

J F M A M J J A S O N D

Male: Black-and-white striped from crown down entire body length; feet and legs charcoal; bill is thin and black with thin yellow line at mouth opening.
Female: Similar to the male except striping on chest and belly is grey and white, throat is white.

Did you know? The Black and White Warbler is one of the earliest migrants to return in spring.

Voice: Seven or more squeaky calls *weesee, weesee, weesee, weesee, weesee, weesee, weesee.*
Food: A variety of insects, mainly gypsy moths and tent caterpillars.
Nest/Eggs: Cup built of leaves, grass, hair and bark, at base of tree or near a boulder. 4-5 eggs.

Nesting Location

Egg: Actual Size

Tennesee Warbler

Vermivora peregrina

Observation Calendar
J F M A M J J A S O N D

Male/Female: Thin, very pointed bill; blue-grey crown; distinct white line over eye; olive back and wings; white underparts.

Voice: High-pitched three-part twitter — *ticka ticka ticka swit swit swit sit sit sit sit sit.*
Food: Insects, especially spruce budworms.
Nest/Eggs: Nest of grasses on the ground, often in sphagnum and other mosses. 4-7 eggs.

Nashville Warbler

Vermivora ruficapilla

Size Identification

Beak

Male/Female: Thin, very pointed bill; head and neck bluish grey; eye-ring white; upper parts olive green; underparts yellow, white on belly.

Voice: Calls include *see it see it see it*, and *ti ti ti ti ti*.
Food: A variety of insects.
Nest/Eggs: Nest of moss or bark lined with grass and hair, on ground. 4-5 eggs.

Nesting Location

113   Egg: Actual Size

Northern Parula Warbler
Parula americana

Observation Calendar

J F M A M J J A S O N D

Male: One of the smallest warblers. Rust colour under chin turning grey at belly and rump; wings and tail feathers black with white edges; small patch of yellow-green on back; legs and feet black; bill is long and thin; two distinct white bars on wings.

Female: Patch on back is duller and belly is light yellow.

Did you know? Parula means "little titmouse." The movements of the Parula Warbler are very similar to the chickadee and the titmouse.

Voice: Repeated song sounding like a twitter which ends in a *yip*.

Food: A variety of insects

Nest/Eggs: Cup of twigs, leaves and moss, hanging in tree branches, 2-30 metres above ground. 3-7 eggs.

Magnolia Warbler

Dendroica magnolia

Beak

J F M A M J J A S O N D

Male: Grey head with small eyebrow stripe of white above eye; black mask; yellow chin; chest and belly yellow with black banding; back grey with black banding; wings and tail grey with white edges; two white wing bars; white rump.
Female: Similar to male except banding on chest is narrower; face is grey without black mask and white eyebrow; white eye ring.

Voice: A short melodic song *weeta weeta weeta wee.*
Food: A variety of insects and spiders.
Nest/Eggs: Loosely built cup nest of grass, moss and weed stalks, lined with dark roots, in small conifers along the edge of wooded areas and in gardens. 3-5 eggs.

Nesting Location

Egg: Actual Size

Black-throated Blue Warbler

Dendroica caerulescens

Size Identification

Beak

Observation Calendar

J F M A M J J A S O N D

Male: Blue-grey head and back; black face mask with black bill; chest white; wings and tail black with white edges; feet and legs black.

Female: Olive-brown head, back and wings with lighter tone on chin, chest and belly; black bill; thin buff eyebrows; feet and legs black; wings and tail olive-brown with white edges.

Voice: A husky song, "I am soo lazzzzy," and a call that is flat *tip*.

Food: A variety of insects, fruits and seeds taken mainly on ground or low lying branches.

Nest/Eggs: Bulky cup of spider's web, dead wood, twigs, leaves and grass, lined with dark rootlets in tree or shrub close to ground. 3-5 eggs.

Nesting Location

Yellow-rumped Warbler

Dendroica coronata

J F M A M J J A S O N D

Male/Female: *Spring:* Yellow rump and yellow patch on either side of chest; yellow crest set against grey head; black mask running from black bill; back grey with black banding; wings and tail black with white edges; two white wing bars; chin white; chest white with black band; feet and legs charcoal; white eyebrow. *Fall:* Similar but duller markers, no black mask, more brown and buff overall.

Did you know? A very abundant warbler that was once called Myrtle Warbler and was thought to be two different species because of its change of plumage.

Voice: Song is light musical notes. Call is *cheeeck.*
Nests: In gardens and conifer forests.
Food: A variety of insects and fruit.
Nest/Eggs: Deep cup of twigs, bark, plant down and fibres, lined with hair feather and fine grass, in tree or shrub near trunk. 3-5 eggs.

Black-throated Green Warbler

Dendroica virens

Beak

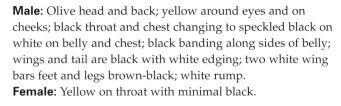

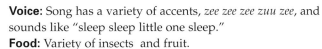

J F M A M J J A S O N D

Male: Olive head and back; yellow around eyes and on cheeks; black throat and chest changing to speckled black on white on belly and chest; black banding along sides of belly; wings and tail are black with white edging; two white wing bars feet and legs brown-black; white rump.
Female: Yellow on throat with minimal black.

Voice: Song has a variety of accents, *zee zee zee zuu zee*, and sounds like "sleep sleep little one sleep."
Food: Variety of insects and fruit.
Nest/Eggs: Compact cup of fine bark, twigs, grass, lichens and spider's web, lined with hair, fur, feathers and small roots, in tree or shrub, 1-25 metres above ground. 3-5 eggs.

Nesting Location

Bay-breasted Warbler

Dendroica castanea

Size Identification

Beak

Observation Calendar

Observation Calendar

J F M A M J J A S O N D

Male: *Spring:* Deep rust patch on top of black head; rust on chin and along sides of chest; grey back with black banding; two white wing bars; wings and tail are black with white edges; belly white with soft rust on sides; rump white; buff patch on either side of neck; feet and legs black with hints of red. *Fall:* head changes to olive/yellow; back is yellow/olive; chest is white with pink on sides, rump is buff.
Female: Duller with less rust on neck and sides.

Did you know? The quickest way to identify the Bay-breasted Warbler is to locate the buff patch on the side of the neck.

Nesting Location

Voice: Difficult to distinguish from other warblers. Song is high pitched *seetsy seetsy seetsy*. Call *see*.
Food: A variety of tree dwelling insects.
Nest/Eggs: Loosely woven cup nest built of twigs, dried grass and spider's web, lined with small roots, hair and fine grasses, in tree or shrub, 4-8 metres above ground. 4-7 eggs.

Egg: Actual Size

Ovenbird
Seiurus aurocapillas

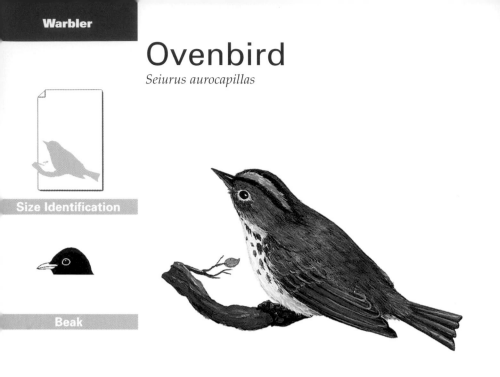

J F M A M J J A S O N D

Male/Female: Olive overall with distinctive mark on head that is orange outlined in black, running from bill to the back of the neck; chest white with black speckles; bill dark on top with yellow on underside; black eyes surrounded by white.

Voice: A progressively louder, *teecher, teecher, teecher, teecher.*
Food: Snails, slugs, worms, spiders and most other insects.
Nest/Eggs: Covered bowl, with side entry made of dead leaves, grass, moss and bark, lined with small roots, fibres and hair, on ground in depression. 3-5 eggs.

Northern Waterthrush

Seiurus noveboracensis

J F M A M J J A S O N D

Male/Female: Brown head and back with distinctive yellow eyebrow running to back of head; chest pale yellow with dark pronounced banding running down to lower belly; legs pink and red; bill black and pink; short tail.

Voice: A ringing song which drops off at the end. Call is a metallic *chink.*

Food: A variety of insects and water bugs, crustaceans, small fish, mollusks.

Nest/Eggs: Cup or dome of moss, twigs, bark and leaves, lined with moss, hair and fine grass on ground in upturned roots or fallen trees. 4-5 eggs.

Mourning Warbler
Oporornis philadelphia

Size Identification

Beak

Observation Calendar

J F M A M J J A S O N D

Male: Grey hood with olive back; yellow chest and belly with black collar; bill black with pale underparts; wings and tail dark with yellow edges; rump yellow; feet and legs brown.
Female: Hood is duller; broken white eye ring; wings and tail olive ending in black with white edges; chest pale grey.

Voice: Loud ringing *chirry chirry chirry chorry.*
Food: A variety of insects and spiders.
Nest/Eggs: Bulky cup of leaves, vines, grass, weeds and bark, lined with fine grasses, rootlets and hair, on or near ground. 3-5 eggs.

Nesting Location

Egg: Actual Size   122

Common Yellowthroat

Geothlypis trichas

Observation Calendar

J F M A M J J A S O N D

Male: Yellow chin, chest and belly contrast with a dark black mask which runs from bill, around eyes to lower neck; white line blends into an olive head, back, wings and tail; feet and legs grey.

Female: Light brown without the distinctive mask.

Voice: A very high—pitched song, *witchity, witchity, witchity,* that is heavily accented.

Food: Caterpillars, beetles, ants and other small insects.

Nest/Eggs: Bulky cup of grass, reeds, leaves and moss, lined with grass and hair, on or near ground, in weed stalks or low bushes. 3-5 eggs.

American Redstart
Setophaga ruticilla

Size Identification

Beak

Backyard Feeder

Observation Calendar
J F M A M J J A S O N D

Male: Black overall with large orange bands on wings and outer tail feathers; bright red/orange patch on side of chest; belly white; feet and legs black.
Female: Overall olive-grey with large yellow bands on wings and tail; white eye-ring, broken; yellow on sides of white chest; white belly; feet and legs black.

Voice: Song is a series of high-pitched thin notes ending downward. Call is *chip*.
Food: A variety of insects, wild berries and seeds.
Nest/Eggs: Compact woven cup built with plant down and grass, lined with weeds, hair and feathers, covered on the outside with lichens, plant down and spider's web, in woodlands and swamps. 4 eggs.

Nesting Location

Egg: Actual Size   124

House Sparrow

Passer domesticus

Beak

Backyard Feeder

Birdhouse Nester

Nesting Location

Observation Calendar

J F M A M J J A S O N D

Male: Rich brown on head with white cheeks; wings and tail striped with black; two distinct white wing bands; rump grey; throat and chest black which turns grey at belly; bill black; feet and legs pink.

Female: Dull brown with buff chin, chest and belly; light buff coloured eyebrows and yellow/grey bill.

Did you know? In the mid-1800s eight pairs of House Sparrows were brought to North America from Europe to help control cankerworms in crops. The first attempt failed but this sparrow has now become one of the most common birds in cities and towns.

Voice: Repeated *chureep, chirup.*
Food: Insects, seed, grain and food waste.
Nest/Eggs: Takes over nests from other birds. Usually a large untidy ball of grass, weeds, some hair, feathers. 3-7 eggs.

125

Bobolink
Dolichonyx oryzivorus

Beak

Observation Calendar

J F M A M J J A S O N D

Male: *Summer:* Black overall with pale yellow patch on back of head; back black changing to large white patch down to rump; wings have white patches and edges; feet, legs, and bill black. In flight: white rump is revealed. Tail has sharp pointed feathers.
Female/Male: *Winter:* brown and buff overall with black streaks over top of head; legs red.

Did you know? These birds need hayfield habitat to survive. Studies show that most young will die when farmers' fields are mown before they have a chance to fledge.

Nesting Location

Voice: Song is a light phrase that increases in pitch and has been described as *Bob o link - bob o link spink spank spink.* Usually sings in flight. Call is metallic *clink.*
Food: A variety of insects and weed seeds.
Nest/Eggs: Slight hollow in ground with bulky gathering of grass and weed stalks. Lined with fine grass in areas near water and within waterside plants. 4-7 eggs.

Red-winged Blackbird
Agelaius phoeniceus

Beak

Backyard Feeder

Observation Calendar

J F M A M J J A S O N D

Male: Black overall with distinctive red shoulder patch bordered with light yellow at bottom.
Female: Brown with buff eyebrows and chin; chest and belly buff streaked with dark brown; wings and tail feathers brown with buff edges.

Did you know? Red-winged Blackbirds are prolific breeders, sometimes breeding three times in one season. They are seen in freshwater marshes throughout the province.

Nesting Location

Voice: Song is *ocaaleee ocaalee.*
Food: A variety of insects and weed seeds.
Nest/Eggs: Bulky cup built of leaves, rushes, grass, rootlets, moss and milkweed fibre, lined with grass, in tall waterside plants near water. 3-4 eggs.

Egg: Actual Size

Common Grackle
Quiscalus quiscula

Size Identification

Beak

Backyard Feeder

Male: Overall iridescent black and purple; bright yellow eye; black bill long and sharp; feet and legs are charcoal grey; long tail.
Female: Similar but duller iridescent colouring, tail is shorter.

Did you know? Flocks in the thousands gather on fields and cause a lot of damage to farmers' crops.

Voice: Chatter is a metallic and rasping *grideleeeeek*. Calls are *chak chah*.
Food: A variety of ground insects, seeds, grain, minnows, rodents and crayfish.
Nest/Eggs: Loose bulky cup built with weed stalks, twigs, grass, debris, lined with feather and grass, in conifer tree or shrubs. Will occasionally use an osprey's nest. Prefers to nest in colonies. 3-6 eggs.

Nesting Location

Egg: Actual Size

128

Brown-headed Cowbird
Molothrus ater

Observation Calendar

J F M A M J J A S O N D

Male: Brown head, glossy black overall; feet and legs black; sharp black bill.
Female: Overall grey with dark brown wings and tail; faint buff streaking on chest down to lower belly, feet and legs are black.

Did you know? Molothrus ater, the Cowbird's scientific name, means dark, greedy beggar, an apt name for a bird that leaves its eggs for other birds to hatch.

Voice: A squeaky *weee titi.*
Nest/Eggs: Lays eggs in nests of other birds. 1 egg.
Food: A variety of insects, weed seeds, grain and grass.

Scarlet Tanager
Piranga olivacea

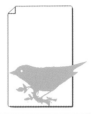

Beak

Observation Calendar
J F M A M J J A S O N D

Male: Scarlet red from head to rump with dark black wings and tail; bill is dull yellow; feet and legs black.
Female: Olive-yellow overall with black-gray wings and tail.

Voice: Call is a Chip burr while its song is a buzzing *querit, queer, queery, querit, queer* that is well spaced out.
Food: A variety of insects and fruit.
Nest/Eggs: Flat and flimsy cup nest on farthest branches in tree or shrub, sometimes far from the ground. 3-5 eggs.

Nesting Location

Rose-breasted Grosbeak

Pheucticus ludovicianus

Observation Calendar

J F M A M J J A S O N D

Male: Large, pale yellow bill with black head; red V shape on chest; belly white with rust on either side; wings and tail black with white at edges of tail feathers visible in flight; white patches on wings; rump white; feet and legs charcoal.
Female: Buff eyebrow that extends to back of neck; brown head and back with shade of black; wings and tail brown with white edges; two white wing bars; chest and belly speckled brown; feet and legs charcoal.

Did you know? The Rose-breasted Grosbeak is a fierce competitor when mating, clashing violently with other males. However, when it comes time to sitting on the nest, the males have been known to sing.

Voice: Similar to a robin but rapid notes that are continuous *cheer-e-ly cheer-e-ly.* Call is *chink chink.*
Food: A variety of insects, tree buds, fruit and wild seeds.
Nest/Eggs: Woven grass cup in fork of deciduous tree or shrub, close to the ground. 3-6 eggs.

Evening Grosbeak
Coccothraustes vespertinus

Size Identification

Beak

Backyard Feeder

Observation Calendar
J F M A M J J A S O N D

Male: Dark brown/black head with dull yellow stripe across forehead that blends into a dull yellow at the shoulders; tail and wings are black with hints of white; chest and stomach, dull yellow; stout pale yellow bill and dark pink feet.
Female: Silver grey with light hints of dull yellow on neck and sides, tail and wings are black with white edges.

Did you know? The Evening Grosbeak was mostly seen in western Canada until recent times when it moved east and north and can now be found in many parts of the Maritimes.

Nesting Location

Voice: Call is a ringing *cleer* or *clee-ip*. When there is a flock of birds calling they sound like sleighbells.
Food: Seeds, insects various fruits and flower buds.
Nest/Eggs: Loosely woven cup of twigs and moss lined with small roots. Conifer tree or shrub, in colonies. 3-4 eggs.

Egg: Actual Size   132

Pine Siskin

Carduelis pinus

Observation Calendar

J F M A M J J A S O N D

Male/Female: Brown with buff chest and belly banded with brown; long pointed bill is grey, wings and tail dark with yellow edges; feet and legs grey

Did you know? Two points of identification of the Pine Siskin are its size and the song, which it sings in flight.

Voice: Light rasping *tit i tit* and louder *cleeeip*. Similar to a Goldfinch but deeper and coarser.
Food: Conifer seeds, weed seeds, nectar, flower buds and a variety of insects.
Nest/Eggs: Large shallow cup built with twigs, grass, moss, lichen, bark and small roots, lined with moss, hair and feathers in a conifer tree well out from trunk, 6 metres above ground. 2-6 eggs.

133

American Goldfinch
Carduelis tristis

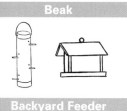

Observation Calendar

J F M A M J J A S O N D

Male: *Summer:* Bright yellow overall with black forehead and yellow bill; black wings with white bands; tail black with white edges; rump white; feet and legs red. *Winter:* Similar yellow is replaced by gray with hints of yellow.
Female/Male: *Winter:* similar except overall olive brown with yellow highlights.

Voice: Sing as they fly with a succession of chips and twitters, *per chic o ree per chic o ree.*
Food: A variety of insects but mostly interested in thistle and weed seeds.
Nest/Eggs: Neat cup built with fibres woven together, lined with thistle and feather down, in leafy tree or shrubs in upright branches, 1-5 metres above ground. 4-6 eggs.

White-winged Crossbill

Loxia leucoptera

Size Identification

Beak

Backyard Feeder

Observation Calendar

J F M A M J J A S O N D

Male: Overall pinkish-red with long black bill that crosses over at the end; wings and tail black, with two large white bars; lower belly turns grey; feet and legs charcoal.
Female: Similar to male except greyish with olive areas on back and head, yellow on chest and rump.

Did you know? Their bills are used to scrap conifer seeds by forcing open the cone and pulling seeds out.

Voice: Call to each other *peeet* with a flight call of *chif chif*.
Food: Conifer seeds, variety of insects and other seeds.
Nest/Eggs: Deep cup built with twig, small roots, weed stalks, moss, lichen, and bark, lined with grass, feather and hair, in spruce tree or shrub, 2-3 metres above ground. 2-5 eggs.

Nesting Location

Egg: Actual Size

Savannah Sparrow

Passerculus sandwichensis

Observation Calendar

J F M A M J J A S O N D

Male/Female: Black, brown and white central stripe on head; back brown with black banding; chin, chest and belly streaked with black and brown; wings and tail black with brown edges; tail is notched; bright yellow eyebrow; feet and legs red; short pointed bill is black and pink; white eye ring.

Voice: A faint, lisping *tsit tsit tsit tseeeee tsaaaay.*
Food: Main diet consist of weed seeds but will eat a variety of insects, spiders and snails.
Nest/Eggs: Scratched hollow in ground filled with grass, lined with finer grass, hair and small roots. 3-6 eggs.

Chipping Sparrow
Spizella passerina

Size Identification

Beak

Backyard Feeder

Observation Calendar

J F M A M J J A S O N D

Male/Female: *Summer:* Bright rust crown with grey face that has a black band running through eye; short pointed bill is black; chin white changing to grey for chest and belly; feet and legs pink with black; white eyebrow; wings and tail black with brown and white edges; back brown banding with black. *Winter:* Rust crown becomes duller turning brown with black streaks; bill is pale yellow and black; eyebrow changes to buff; underside changes to buff.

Voice: Song is short trill.
Food: A variety of insects on the ground and occasionally snatches flying insects.
Nest/Eggs: Cup built with grass, weed stalks and small roots, lined with hair and grass, low in tree or shrub, up to 8 metres above ground. 4 eggs.

Nesting Location

Egg: Actual Size

Song Sparrow
Melospiza lincolnii

Size Identification

Beak

Backyard Feeder

Observation Calendar

J F M A M J J A S O N D

Male/Female: Brown head and back streaked with black; buff-grey eyebrow extending to back of neck; brown band running through eye; chin, chest and belly are white with brown-black banding running down to lower belly; short pointed bill is black on top with yellow underside; red-brown crown with central white stripe; wings and tail brown with white edges; feet and legs pink; long rounded tail.

Did you know? Thoreau 'interpreted' this sparrow's song as "Maids! Maids! Maids! hang up your teakettle-ettle-ettle."

Nesting Location

Voice: Call is a variety which includes *tsip* and *tchump*. Song is a variety of rich notes.
Food: A variety of insects, weed seeds and fruit.
Nest/Eggs: Cup close to ground with weeds, leaves and bark, lined with grass roots and hair, in tree or shrub, less than 4 metres from ground. 3-5 eggs.

Egg: Actual Size   138

Dark-eyed Junco
Junco hyemalis

Size Identification

Beak

Backyard Feeder

Observation Calendar

J F M A M J J A S O N D

Male: Dark charcoal overall with white belly; short sharp bill is pale yellow with black at end; feet and legs dark grey; tail has white outer feathers that can be seen in flight.
Female: May be slightly paler than male.

Did you know? Although there are many different sub-species, the slate-coloured species is the only one found in the region.

Voice: Song is a trill in short phrases. Calls are *tsip, zeeet* or *keew keew.*
Food: A variety of insects, weed seeds and wild fruit.
Nest/Eggs: Large and compact built with grass, rootlets and hair, lined with hair, concealed low to or on ground. 4-5 eggs.

Nesting Location

139

Egg: Actual Size

White-throated Sparrow

Zonotrichia albicollis

Size Identification

Beak

Backyard Feeder

Observation Calendar

J F M A M J J A S O N D

Male/Female: Top of head is black with white central stripe; white eyebrows on either side that begin with yellow tint; black band running through eye followed by grey cheeks; small white bib under chin; grey chest; white belly with faint banding; wings and tail feathers black and brown with white edges; feet pink; back brown banded with black.

Voice: Whistle is *teeet teeet tetodi tetodi teetodi.* Calls are *tseet.*
Food: A variety of insects, grain, weed seeds and fruit.
Nest/Eggs: Cup built of grass, small roots, pine needles, twigs, bark and moss, lined with small roots, hair and grass. 3-5 eggs.

Nesting Location

Swamp Sparrow
Melospiza georgiana

Beak

Observation Calendar
J F M A M J J A S O N D

Male/Female: *Summer:* Top of head is reddish brown and black; face grey with black streaks; black bill is small and sharp; chin and chest white-grey with rust along sides; back brown with black banding; wings and tail feathers brown with black ends and white edges; feet and legs pink; grey eyebrows. *Winter:* Similar to summer but both sides of chest turn darker brown and top of head is streaked with black and brown with grey central stripe.

Put on your hip waders to spot this bird. They spend their summers near swamps and bogs.

Voice: Song is an unbroken musical trill. Call is *chip.*
Food: A variety of insects and seeds.
Nest/Eggs: Bulky cup built with grass, lined with finer grass, in tussock of grass or in low shrub. 3-6 eggs.

Nesting Location

141   Egg: Actual Size

2-Step Bird Finder

Step 1. Determine the approximate size of bird in relation to page size.
Step 2. Compare overall colour and specific markings and turn to the page number.

Bittern, American 20
Blackbird, Red-winged, 127;
    also Bobolink, 126;
    Brown-headed Cowbird,
    129; Common Grackle,
    128
Bobolink, 126
Brant, 22
Bufflehead, 33

Canada Goose, 21
Cedar Waxwing, 108
Chickadee, Black-capped,
    100; Boreal, 101
Cormorant, Double-crested,
    18; Great, 17
Cowbird, Brown-headed, 129
Crossbill, White-winged, 135
Crow, American, 99

Double-crested Cormorant,
    18
Dove, Mourning, 80; Rock,
    79]
Dowitcher, Short-billed, 68
Duck, American Black, 24;
    Long-tailed, 34; Ring-
    necked, 30; Wood, 29;
    also, American Wigeon,
    28; Black Scoter, 38; Blue-
    winged Teal, 27;
    Bufflehead, 33; Common
    Eider, 35; Common
    Goldeneye, 32; Greater
    Scaup, 31; Green-winged
    Teal, 26; Mallard, 23;
    Northern Pintail, 25; Surf
    Scoter, 37; White-winged
    Scoter, 36

Eagle, Bald, 43
Eider, Common, 35
Evening Grosbeak, 132

Finch; see American
    Goldfinch, 134; Pine
    Siskin, 133
Flycatcher, Least, 91

Gannet, Northern, 16
Golden-crowned Kinglet, 106
Goldeneye, Common, 32
Goldfinch, American, 134
Goose, Canada, 21; also
    Brant, 22
Grackle, Common 128
Gray Partridge, 48
Great Black-backed Gull, 71
Great Blue Heron, 19
Great Cormorant, 17
Great Horned Owl, 81
Greater Scaup, 31
Greater Yellowlegs, 61
Grebe, Horned, 14; Pied-
    billed, 15
Grosbeak, Evening, 132;

Rose-breasted, 131
Grouse, 47
Gull, Bonaparte's, 74; Great
    Black-backed, 71;
    Herring, 72; Iceland, 70;
    Ring-billed, 73

Hawk, Marsh, 44; Sharp-
    shinned, 42
Heron, Great Blue, 19
Hummingbird, Ruby-throat-
    ed, 86

Jay, Blue, 97
Junco, Dark-eyed, 139

Kestrel, American, 46
Killdeer, 53
Kingbird, Eastern, 90
Kingfisher, Belted, 87
Kinglet, Golden-crowned,
    106; Ruby-crowned, 107
Knot, Red, 63

Lark, Horned, 93
Loon, Common, 12; Red-
    throated, 13

Mallard, 23
Merganser, Common, 39;
    Hooded, 41; Red-breast-
    ed, 40
Mourning Dove, 80

Nuthatch, Red-breasted, 102

Osprey, 45
Ovenbird, 120
Owl, Barred, 83; Great
    Horned, 81; Northern
    Saw-whet, 85; Short
    Eared, 84; Snowy, 82

Partridge, 48
Phalarope, Red-necked, 69
Pheasant, Ring-necked, 49
Pigeon, 79
Pine Siskin, 133
Plover, Black-bellied, 54;
    Semipalmated, 51;
    Piping, 52; also Killdeer,
    53
Puffin, Atlantic, 78

Raven, 98
Redstart, American, 124
Robin, American, 103
Rock Dove, 79
Ruddy Turnstone, 55
Ruffed Grouse, 47

Sanderling, 67
Sandpiper, Least, 65;
    Pectoral, 64;
    Semipalmated, 66;
    Spotted, 59
Sapsucker, Yellow-bellied, 88
Scoter, Black, 38; Surf, 37;
    White-winged, 36

Snipe, Common, 57
Sora, 50
Sparrow, Chipping, 137;
    House, 125; Savannah,
    136; Song, 138; Swamp,
    141; White-throated, 140
Starling, 109
Swallow, Bank, 95; Barn, 96;
    Tree, 94

Tanager, Scarlet, 130
Teal, Blue-winged, 27;
    Green-winged, 26
Tern, Arctic, 76; Caspian, 77;
    Common, 75
Thrush, Hermit, 104;
    Swainson's, 105; also
    American Robin, 103
Turnstone, 55

Vireo, Red-eyed, 110

Warbler, Bay-breasted, 119;
    Black-and-White, 111;
    Black-throated Blue, 116;
    Black-throated Green,
    118; Magnolia, 115;
    Mourning, 122;
    Nashville, 113; Northern
    Parula, 114; Tennessee,
    112; Yellow-rumped, 117;
    also American Redstart,
    124; Common
    Yellowthroat, 123;
    Northern Waterthrush,
    121; Ovenbird, 120
Waterthrush, Northern, 121
Waxwing, 108
Whimbrel, 58
Willet, 60
Wigeon, American, 28
Woodcock, American, 56
Woodpecker, Downy, 89
Wood-peewee, Eastern, 92

Yellowlegs, Greater, 61;
    Lesser, 62